'TWEEN 9 'n 15

TARIQ HAMEED

JUST ROAMING IN THE DARK ... ADOLESCENCE
WHEN DONE'S DONE, THEN DONE 'TWERE 'NER UNDONE

AuthorHouse™ UK
1663 Liberty Drive
Bloomington, IN 47403 USA
www.authorhouse.co.uk
UK TFN: 0800 0148641 (Toll Free inside the UK)
UK Local: 02036 956322 (+44 20 3695 6322 from outside the UK)

This book is printed on acid-free paper.

ISBN: 978-1-6655-9027-3 (sc)
ISBN: 978-1-6655-9026-6 (e)

Print information available on the last page.

Published by AuthorHouse 08/19/2021

Publishing Planned: 05/05/2021	2nd. book	**Completion: 14/08/2021**
(Kublai Khan's Coronation ... 05/05/1260)	'tween 9 'n 15	**(Pak Independence ... 14/08/1947)**
Publishing Planned: 21/02/2021	1st. book	**Completion: 05/05/2021**
(Mother's Goodbye-World Anniversary ... '72)	Kublai Khan	**(Kublai Coronation ... 05/05/1260)**

History of **Urdu** ... The **Mongol**/Turkish word **Urdu** means "**Camp**" or "**Palace**" ... Kublai ...

... **The Final Place of Rest** ... And That's How My Poëm Ends: Sadly ...

Awaiting; that the Loose last breath, be shed,
'N downed he slept: Camp Urdu in bed,
That Spirits to the Ninth Heaven Arise.

Introduction ... by Tariq Hameed ... A bit about my Child-h◉-◉d!

A Voracious Reader; Underlined Un-Underst◉-◉d, in **Black**, then Green, then **Red** ... till **Dictionary by Heart**! Was Myopic: Friends t◉-◉k me as Proud: NO Recognition? So,, I Learnt to Measure Persons, by **Movements**! **Dreams remain Dreams** ... Till True Today? Thus,, my **Ears**, **Nose**, **Tongue** 'n **Thoughts** ... became my **Mind**!

Set is the Stage, the Play? Captured by a total Un-Known Future? Energy, Education, Evolution, Evade, Earth!

TOTAL respect of All 'n Others, was my Device ... Friends, Masters, Country-men 'n Un-Country-men: 'n **All**!

1st. Step: **Sch◉-◉l** ... **Be in Bed by 9**? Couldn't Read! Contrived an Invention; **Wires**, **Cells**, 'n **Lil Lamps**; thus Read in the Dark, **inside my Quilt** ... Read 250 pages: till Late Midnight: 'bout 5000 B◉-◉ks: to 10 yrs.
2nd. Step: Sch◉-◉l ... **Myopic**? Couldn't Read the Black-Board ... So, Ô Chalk's Sound 'n Moving Fingers: Be My Guides? Every Move was Revelation 'n Indication! **What 'twas being Said 'n Writ**? Thus Knew All.
3rd. Step: **College** ... **Summary Master**? Start by Diction: Who Finished 1st. could leave the Class-R◉-◉m ... So, Instead of Noting the Text, I Wrote Directly the Summary: **Never** was I Beat to Finish ... to Leave Class!

Homages ... by Myself ... to my Masters ... who Built me Future

1. **My Mother** ... 'Mongst 1st. **Lady Doctors** (India) ... Gave me 100 Words to Memorise by Day ... **NO Errors**!
   Thus aged 9, I knew the English Dictionary by Heart! **A Voracious Reader** ... I Noted Every Word read!
2. **My Father** ... Titled "**Khan Sahib**" by ***Exiting British***, for Services Rendered to *Election Laws* ... He Wrote,
   in 1952, "**Election Law**" for Pakistan ... which is still a **Reference Book**, in the **Supreme Court**!
3. **My Uncle** ... **Scribe** 'n **Hafiz**-e-Qura'an ... till Aged 20, Instructed me "**Atomic Letters**", in **Urdu** 'n English;
   Letter, **Dot**, **Accent** Separated: that 60 years later, I created the "**Atomic** Wrist **Key-Board**"!
4. **My Servitor** ... **Ashraf** the Cross-Eyed; who Saw Nothing, **but** Knew Everything: Known 'n Unknown!
   Excellent Story-Teller ... His Legend of "**Ogre Khumra and the Rosy Færy**", NEVER ended all 20 years!
5. **My Musician** ... Feroz **Nizami** ... Sweet, Soft 'n Classical ... Created the Best Pak Film Tunes, in 50-tys
6. **My Theatre Writer** ... Syed Imtiaz Ali Taj ... Historical Personality ... *Died in my Arms*: **God Bless U**!
7. **My Loved Poët** ... Faiz Ahmed Faiz ... Poetry Lenin Prize, 1962! **Spoke** but little: **Smoked** but much!
8. **My Best Friend** ... Tanvir Ahmed **Khan** ... Born a day after, 77 years Perfect ... in **Respect Respected**!
9. **My Calligrapher Adored** ... Ahmed Mirza Jamil ... "Think NOT with Brain; **Think with Wrist**: Tariq"!

(2000)

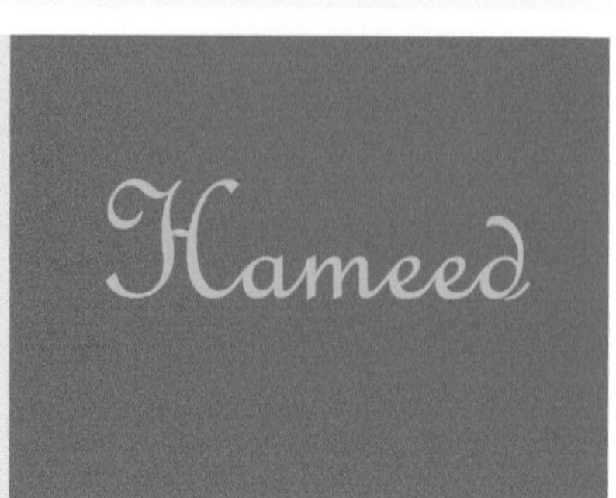

Voracious **Reader 'n Searcher**, since **Two 'n Half years Old**, of Where **LIES** the **TRUTH**?

"**Aye, there lies the rub**": so in this **Hamlet of No Return**, called '**World of the Wise of Gotham**', only but to be so Bed-Ridden by the **Un-Wise of Bottom**, my small Wisdom but Swore faintly; "**Never Truly Grow-up**"!

'Twas Destiny, that born Myopic, forced me to **Imagine**. Thus, Truth 'n Purity came to Grasp: it a day dawned that, "Dirt were you Born, to returnest to Dirt" ... **Empty-Handed Come, 'n Empty-Handed Gone** ... thus lil by lil, formed a Philosophy: "**You only GAIN, what you GIVE**"! Help Humanity; Not your own Self-Self!

Thus learning early, that **Seeing was Un-Truth** ... Lampions big of Light, Blinking 'n Flickering, so Blown-up in Multi-Fluid Colours in the Deep Depths of the Cosmos' ... factually were, **Else-Things in Else-Where**? Questions to be Posed 'n Answered: allowing the use of other Senses, like Sounds, Taste, Smell 'n Movements, to Re-construct the feasible **Probable Reality**; intuitively analysing the crayoned cricks 'n cracks of chalky traits, I justly Heard, the Black-Board Talk back to me: 'n Revealed by Magic, the **Writing on the Wall** ...

so Un-Veiled, the False-ho-od of the **Persons of Convenience**?

42. (Vaticano) **S W A L L O W S** *no punctuation* Visions-3- 1993 Org. thBk-E-5b p-53--152-

a swarm **of**

swallows behind a **swarm** of *swallows* and

could be pointed out in every individual *swallow* which followed ***its***

own individual path and its own individual destiny but at the ***same***

instant become part of a screen of smoke of a big *swarm* ***of***

swallows which twisted and turned in thicker **and thinner veils and veins**

of smoky squirling columns against a **totally poised grey sky in all**

intertranspercing to mingle separate

destinies into a common destiny

permitting to exist not lone

or lonely but as a

compact mass

sometimes

massive

some

time

'tween nine 'n fifteen

… New **Writ** Technique Perusal **Scan/Read** … VIBGYOR … RAINBOW … **Words** in a **Page** only : in a ½ **Minute** …

Book **1** **Volume 1**

Volume I … (Written 'tween 9 & 15 of age) …

… 1951 ➔➔➔ 1957 …

English is myne Mystress … Tariq HAMEED

(**Beowulf**) … An Anglo-Saxon EPIC Poëm …

Dedicated to :

… A R O S Y PETAL … in Fairness 'n Fascination …

… A DESIRE 'n A DREAM … that'll Find Me … Never Ever …

or perhaps

to Know to Learn to Live ? do then Try„ to Read my Books !!!

Without any Harm„ nor to **Self**, nor to **NoOne** !!! Sans faire Mal ni à **Soi**„ ni à **Personne** !

Please Study Page -64--**99**- **for** 'pause' („)… 'tween 9 'n 15 *thBk-E-01*9-15*.pdf

THINKS 'n THOUGHTS

'tween nine 'n fifteen

Book 01 LIVRE 01

My Father died, on

the 16th. of January 1957 (Lahore)

It was the 9th. Birthday of my Brother ... *who*

Innocently Clapped Hands and Asked for his Present ?

He got none ! **(. . . *Then I stopped writing . . . till 1966 . . .*)**

= =

MY PHILOSOPHY

IN LIFE

…

EVERYONE'S GUILTY

UNLESS

PROVED INNOCENT

…

THUS

I HAVE

NEVER

SUFFERED

IN THIS WORLD

MA PHILOSOPHIE

EN VIE

…

TOUS COUPABLES

SI NON

PROUVÉ INNOCENT

…

AINSI

JE N'AI

JAMAIS

SOUFFERT

EN CE MONDE

… What They Taught Me: 'n How …

My Father … Election Commissioner: received many **P**olitical **P**arties **P**resents; all **P**ervaded without **P**ity! 'Twas strictly forbidden, to All 'n One, to touch anything in-coming! Once I took an Orange 'n **P**aid by 3 days **P**reclusion: without food!
Thus, learnt I … **the 11th. Commandment** … THOU shalt **NOT** CHEAT thy EAT!

My Mother … 1st. Lady Doctors, of the Continent: one day, she murmured in the kitchen, with a school-mate; so asked, what 'twas? "You owe him 3 cents"! "I owe **No-Thing** to **No-One**? Pay, 'n I jump 10 meters"! Him sent off, she asked, "Why Risk your Life, son"? "Or I Respect what you Taught me? Or am Lier? Both Ways, such Life's NOT worth Living!
Thus, learnt I … **the 12th. Commandment** … THOU shalt **NOT** SELL thy SOUL!

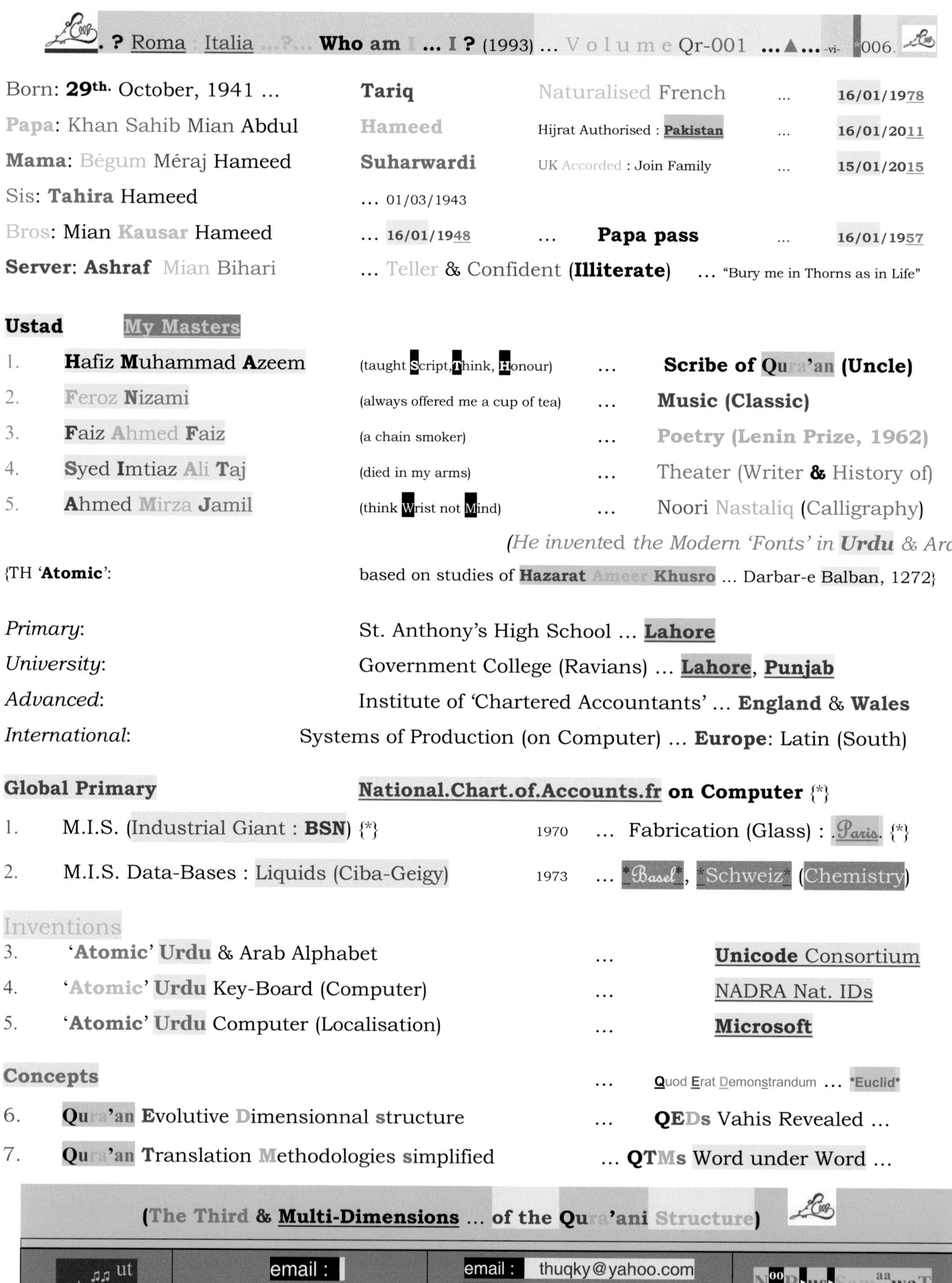

Born: **29th.** October, 1941 ...	**Tariq**	Naturalised French	...	**16/01/1978**
Papa: Khan Sahib Mian Abdul	**Hameed**	Hijrat Authorised : **Pakistan**	...	**16/01/2011**
Mama: Bégum Méraj Hameed	**Suharwardi**	UK Accorded : Join Family	...	**15/01/2015**
Sis: **Tahira** Hameed	... 01/03/1943			
Bros: Mian **Kausar** Hameed	... **16/01/1948**	... **Papa pass**	...	**16/01/1957**
Server: **Ashraf** Mian Bihari	... Teller & Confident (**Illiterate**)	... "Bury me in Thorns as in Life"		

Ustad **My Masters**

1. **Hafiz Muhammad Azeem** (taught Script, Think, Honour) ... **Scribe of Qura'an (Uncle)**
2. Feroz **Nizami** (always offered me a cup of tea) ... **Music (Classic)**
3. **Faiz** Ahmed **Faiz** (a chain smoker) ... **Poetry (Lenin Prize, 1962)**
4. **Syed Imtiaz** Ali **Taj** (died in my arms) ... Theater (Writer **&** History of)
5. **Ahmed** Mirza **Jamil** (think Wrist not Mind) ... Noori Nastaliq (Calligraphy)

*(He invented the Modern 'Fonts' in **Urdu** & Arab)*

{TH '**Atomic**': based on studies of **Hazarat Ameer Khusro** ... Darbar-e Balban, 1272}

Primary: St. Anthony's High School ... **Lahore**
University: Government College (Ravians) ... **Lahore**, **Punjab**
Advanced: Institute of 'Chartered Accountants' ... **England** & **Wales**
International: Systems of Production (on Computer) ... **Europe**: Latin (South)

Global Primary **National.Chart.of.Accounts.fr on Computer** {*}

1. M.I.S. (Industrial Giant : **BSN**) {*} 1970 ... Fabrication (Glass) : Paris. {*}
2. M.I.S. Data-Bases : Liquids (Ciba-Geigy) 1973 ... *Basel*, *Schweiz* (Chemistry)

Inventions

3. '**Atomic**' **Urdu** & Arab Alphabet ... **Unicode** Consortium
4. '**Atomic**' **Urdu** Key-Board (Computer) ... NADRA Nat. IDs
5. '**Atomic**' **Urdu** Computer (Localisation) ... **Microsoft**

Concepts ... Quod Erat Demonstrandum ... *Euclid*

6. **Qura'an** Evolutive Dimensionnal structure ... **QEDs** Vahis Revealed ...
7. **Qura'an** Translation Methodologies simplified ... **QTMs** Word under Word ...

(The Third & Multi-Dimensions ... of the Qura'ani Structure)

ut ♫♫ ♫uhu | email : harf.noor@gmail.com | email : thuqky@yahoo.com email : thuqky@gmail.com | NooRus Samaa waT

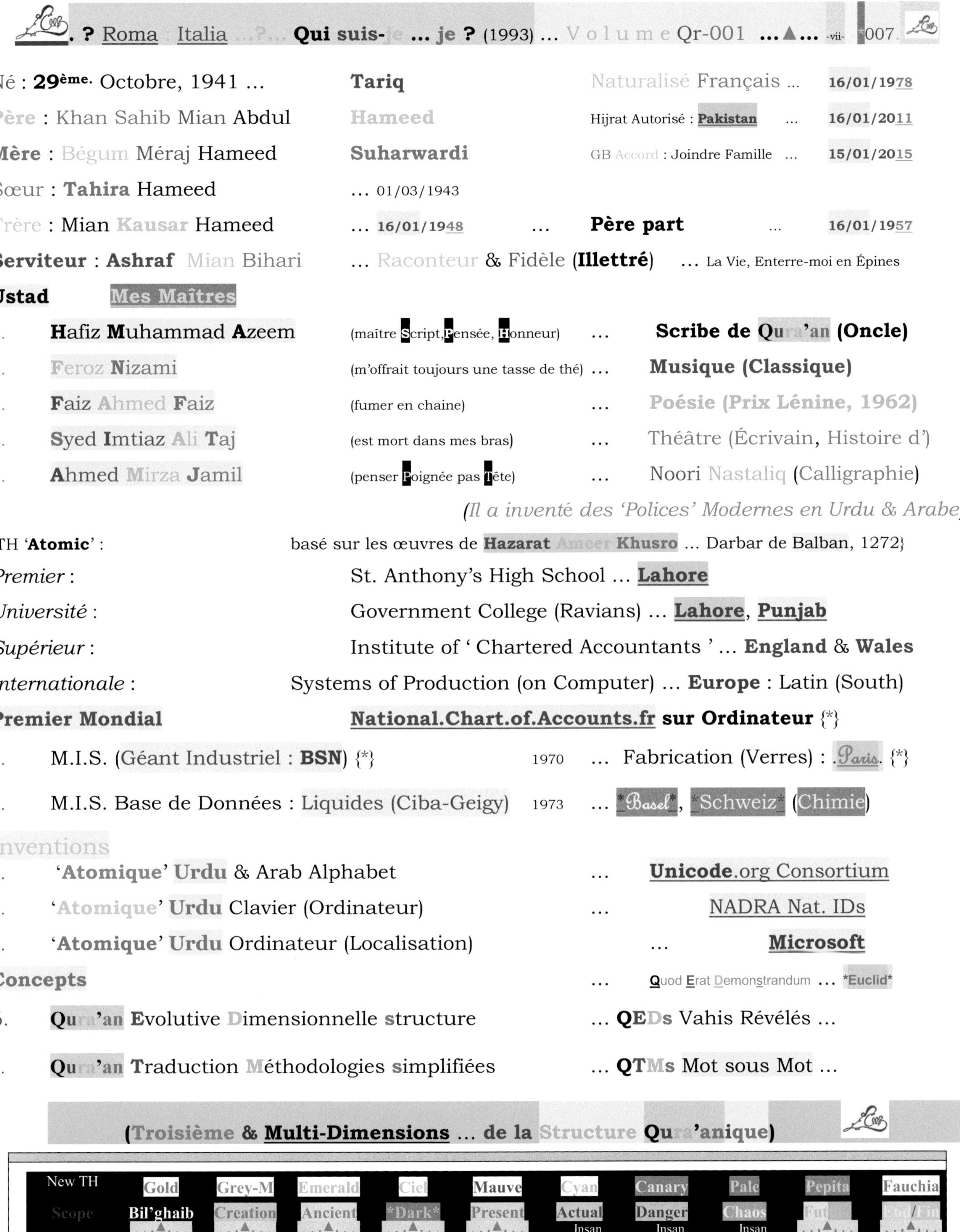

Né : **29ème.** Octobre, 1941 ... **Tariq** Naturalisé Français ... **16/01/1978**

Père : Khan Sahib Mian Abdul **Hameed** Hijrat Autorisé : **Pakistan** ... **16/01/2011**

Mère : Bégum Méraj Hameed **Suharwardi** GB Accord : Joindre Famille ... **15/01/2015**

Sœur : **Tahira** Hameed ... 01/03/1943

Frère : Mian **Kausar** Hameed ... **16/01/1948** ... **Père part** ... **16/01/1957**

Serviteur : **Ashraf** Mian Bihari ... Raconteur & Fidèle (**Illettré**) ... La Vie, Enterre-moi en Épines

Ustad **Mes Maîtres**

1. **Hafiz Muhammad Azeem** (maître Script, Pensée, Honneur) ... **Scribe de Qura'an (Oncle)**
2. **Feroz Nizami** (m'offrait toujours une tasse de thé) ... **Musique (Classique)**
3. **Faiz Ahmed Faiz** (fumer en chaine) ... **Poésie (Prix Lénine, 1962)**
4. **Syed Imtiaz Ali Taj** (est mort dans mes bras) ... Théâtre (Écrivain, Histoire d')
5. **Ahmed Mirza Jamil** (penser Poignée pas Tête) ... Noori Nastaliq (Calligraphie)

(Il a inventé des 'Polices' Modernes en Urdu & Arabe)

{TH '**Atomic**' : basé sur les œuvres de **Hazarat Ameer Khusro** ... Darbar de Balban, 1272}

Premier : St. Anthony's High School ... **Lahore**

Université : Government College (Ravians) ... **Lahore**, **Punjab**

Supérieur : Institute of ' Chartered Accountants ' ... **England** & **Wales**

Internationale : Systems of Production (on Computer) ... **Europe** : Latin (South)

Premier Mondial **National.Chart.of.Accounts.fr sur Ordinateur** {*}

1. M.I.S. (Géant Industriel : **BSN**) {*} 1970 ... Fabrication (Verres) : .Paris. {*}
2. M.I.S. Base de Données : Liquides (Ciba-Geigy) 1973 ... *Basel*, *Schweiz* (Chimie)

Inventions

3. '**Atomique**' **Urdu** & Arab Alphabet ... **Unicode**.org Consortium
4. '**Atomique**' **Urdu** Clavier (Ordinateur) ... NADRA Nat. IDs
5. '**Atomique**' **Urdu** Ordinateur (Localisation) ... **Microsoft**

Concepts ... Quod Erat Demonstrandum ... *Euclid*

6. **Qura'an** **Evolutive** **D**imensionnelle **structure** ... **QEDs** Vahis Révélés ...
7. **Qura'an** **Traduction** **M**éthodologies **s**implifiées ... **QTMs** Mot sous Mot ...

(Troisième & Multi-Dimensions ... de la Structure Qura'anique)

New TH	Gold	Grey-M	Emerald	Ciel	Mauve	Cyan	Canary	Pale	Pepita	Fauchia
Scope	Bil'ghaib	Creation	Ancient	*Dark*	Present	Actual	Danger	Chaos	Fut	End/Fin
	▲I-I ▲ I-I▲	▲I-I ▲ I-I▲	▲I-I ▲ I-I▲	▲I-I ▲ I-I▲	▲I-I ▲ I-I▲	Insan	Insan	Insan	▲I-I ▲ I-I▲	▲I-I ▲ I-I▲
Created	.0. Pure	.1. Attrib	.2. Pro-N	.3. .3. .3.	.4. Conj.	.5. Verb	.6. Concept	.7. .7.	.8.8.8.8.8.	.9. Evil
R G B	128,128,000	128,128,128	000,255,000	000,255,255	200,000,200	100200200	200,255,200	255,100,200	255,200,100	255,100,200

0. *Basel* : *Schweiz* **Surprisingly** (1993)

Written in the age of the early teens,
these are startling impressions when I found them
at forty ... by an accidental command of destiny's design.

The difficult word was my passion then,
my reason to be ... learned ... when young:
which has now changed to the easy word,
my reason to be ... heard ... so old !

Info : 1981 ... **Tariq Hameed**

It is interesting to note that at this age I was extremely myopic but refused to wear corrective glasses. Visually everything impressed me as blurred blots of strangely imprecise colours: as such I resorted to other means for precise understanding and comprehension. I started to *analyse* **senses and sensations** and very often my descriptions are simply based on ***how*** things are **perceived**, rather than ***what*** is **perceived**. Thus, all senses are mingled„ that in the end, All's **Introversion** ... ALL becomes ONE ... the perfect **UNITY** ...

in this manner, the humane body is fully used
and consequently *impregnates itself with knowledge,*
instead of ***simply knowing knowledge, un-knowledged*** *!*
Thus in perception, all senses are unified ... composed and recomposed ...

... Surprisingly Specific ...

Dedication

... To my **Rosy** ... She was all **Rose** ...

Rosy in Heart, **Rosy** in **F**ace, **Rosy** in **Spirit**, **Rosy** in **Soul** ...

So **L**ived my **Rosy** in my **B**eing ... **Rosy** Forgotten 'ner ...

Was she, or was not ... One'll never know ...

... Roma : Italia

This is a Bo-ok on BEAUTY

(1993)

This is a bo-ok on Beauty
written with Beauty.
So please DO NOT read it
if you cannot beautify your life
or live on with beauty.
This is also a bo-ok on human beings
beautiful people who can become better:
It shows no ways no methods
but it can Hopefully make you feel deep inside
that you can be better and much better
than you probably are or have been;
ONLY willing.

There is absolutely NO violence in it.
So please DO NOT read it
if you try your best
NOT to be better.

Unfortunately, to become known, since commerce is now
Our Sole Soul, Dearly, very dearly;
This bo-ok must be published: and costs are costs,
(So any publisher), if not wholly and purely and
totally and plurally insane,
would want his money back;

Hard! But it's not his fault! Pity! None's fault!
Sincerely I apologize for it! And I am very sorry;
it's not my fault either:

Not am I of man, who made the Rules of Mankind!
So please DO NOT buy it, specially
if you have NO excess of money.

Probably, one fine day, a dear fine friend
will loan it to you
in moments of loneliness
this handsomely lonesome bo-ok on Beauty
with Beauty:
so respecting **Po-ored** Beauty
and (my bo-ok on Beauty Abandoned!) Dear, dear friend!

But one day if I can, I will gift it ... free; yes free!
To you ... and the world ... of Shackles and Jackel's-Hides ... free and free and free ...

... *(p.s.* ***2016*** *... by modern means ... I've put it on* *www* *...* ***W****ao* ***W****e'r* ***W****eak ... hi hi ... Quote, but plz, just acknowledge author's name)* ...

1. Qalat : **Baluchistan** **A Tale from Life** (**9 years** – 1950 Aug.) **My First Story** …

*'Twas **Nobody** when born: 'n all bound to live,*
*Cherishing what **D**estiny lent; only later back to give.*

Away spread the **M**ountains, all **W**ildy 'n craggéd.
A child's eye romped well 'n well o'er many a **R**ock raggéd,
o'er many a deep **R**ocky Vale 'n o'er many a high **H**ill **C**lifféd;
all going o'er so up 'n so down, so up 'n so downéd.
*But all was **barren**, **barren brown**.*
He looked away in disgust,,
but beheld a child fair 'n sweet!
She had ruby **L**ips 'n **rosy** **c**heeks:
her **Hair** round her **f**ace curled out neat.
He dreamt **barren** **R**ocks in hardened streaks
flowered to blooming **B**lossoms
'n crevices **B**lossomed to blooms,,
Brown Vales to velvet Meadows turned,,
Swaying Clovers clung forever to evergreen **Trees** forever greened,
And a soft **breeze** did sing
to spray again a **silver** Stream
of this a spurting Spring.
He met her and spoke so sweet **W**ords;
that she raised her shy **e**yes 'n bit her **rosy** **L**ip:
And when they parted, furtive glances each casting behind did slip!

They met again; when he held her **h**and 'n stole a soft kiss!
She **whispered** a low protest; but in all, all in vain … ô miss, ô miss!
Then the first fuzzy snowflakes, when fell as will;
*their gay foot-steps roamed o'er a **lonely** **H**ill.*

The chilly Winds
of freezy **breezy** Winter blew,
The snowy fluffy flakes fell 'n flew
piling up onto the **brown** 'n baring **M**ounts.
So amidst **dark** **Skies** reared up more 'n more
white blanketed **Ghosts** of pleasing things before.
Even **Nature** had donned a cloak of **Melancholy**:
for he was leaving her a-**lonely**!
No **W**ords were said, no **e**yes un-brim-full!
He turned his **f**ace that his welling ***Tear***-drops not be seen.
Down the hateful lane went then he; for never to return.

He wept quietly and through a blur of Streaming *Tears*, ô a Shimmer
imagined, a stunned *Tear*–stained **f**ace did Glimmer.
He wept 'n kissed the **rose**, that which had been her farewell present
She wore it at her lapelled coat
and had snatched at it, just the last moment
'n even though the **rose** was so artificial a bringer,
a cruel Thorn pricked her so tender a **f**inger:
… 'n then she hurried away her way.

Thus he looked out 'n away, far away,
Through a haze of flakes a-falling and *Tears* a-flowing,
'hind the doomed Vale that now stood so hollow,
were craggy Wild Mountains covered with snow.
Years trudged by
'n the child had grown to a man,
Those child-hood fancies as flirtful puffs of air had been blown away.
The **M**emory of hazy brown Mountains had faded to mist,,
but in their midst stood still etched,
in crisps of **S**moke, a Vision, a **L**ovely girl,,
her locks ***S****trayed about her færy-face in a twirl.*
Far from the so Wild
Mountains he grew to a man:
Thru around him lay a hustle 'n a bustle
'n blundered he a hither 'n a thither.
There he sought her everywhere!
The days wore on.
Then at **Night** he pondered,, and when the fresh raindrops fell,
the **lonely** roads echoed his solitary foot-falls to dwell.
These street–**Lamps** cast a dim diffuse **LIGHT**
which mingled with the **darkness** beyond all **Night**
and **Melancholy Reflections Glimmered** on:
Though by the road–side stood yew–Trees all **alone**,
of rain–soaked Barks and dripping **leaves** left **lone**, **alone**.
Thoughts gone on his lapel,, he wore where her **rose** so near 'n close
and still until the end, he searched on onwards on.
Then Spring **came**
and green anew grew the grass;
Flowers Sprouted
all around and **Birds** sang:
'cause he had found her,,
'n found her, at last!

Happy days, happy weeks, happy months flew by;
joyous twinkling **e**yes scattered **Love**
anywhere they a**lighted**.
They roamed everywhere:
but in the stifling **heat** she lay down
in a tired **slumber**;
An innocent **slumber**, deep as if in Death!
*He spake soft **W**ords,, she did not reply;*
he spoke in low caressing tones
and she did not reply:
On her **L**ips he planted a sweet kiss,, but she replied not!
He wore a **S**orrowful look and lowered his wet **e**ye!
And when the auburn Autumn came
and left the rusty **branches** bare,,
Amid the sighs of the scattered **leaves**
reverberated the faint tolling of the distant bell;
The sad notes of a **flute** trickled and **Flickered**
from far away forlorn færy-lands forgotten!
He had **L**ost his **Love** and **L**ost her for **Ever** … in **Never**!
He searched in vain,
all over in vain, but still he searched on … 'n on!
Years have slipped by
and who was once a happy child
is grown to a tired old man: ô man.
His **Hopes** carried along a swift seething Stream
have been swept o'er the rumbling tumbling rapids so low, ô ho ho
'n dashed onto the ***B**roken* **R**ocks below.
*The faded **M**emory of dim hazy **M**ountains floats away*
and from the depths a **cloudy** mist arises: a dear **f**ace peers always out!
A **LIGHT** **W**ind shifts,, there's a turmoil and in their midst … slowly ô so slowly … a few **W**ords appear,
*beside the enchanting **f**ace*
ô **"This is L**ife**!"**
And the echoes form,
The **L**ife **Wheel** spins,, in new 'n newer threads,, 'n out 'n out ô brief out, but ô old so one,
The weak being snapped in their prime,,
And hence, on 'n on and ever on 'n on and on 'n ever on 'n for ever on …

So 'tis **A Tale from Life**,,

'n Constantly, just so Finding 'n Loosing … the very Theme of **L**ife!

"L**ife **gone goes by … for never ever back to come in strife"

1. Qalat : **Baluchistan** **A Tale from Life** (9 years – 1950 Aug.) My First Story …

https://www.pexels.com/search/balochistan%20Pakistan/ … pexels-photo-415969.jpeg … pexels-photo-815880.jpeg

In earlier times, known as Qalat-e-Seva (name of legendary a Hindu king); also Qalat-e-Nicari, in connection with an ancient Brahui dialect Speaking Baloch tribe … one of the oldest branches of the old traditionally indigenous Brahois!

Brahui Speaking Balochis, arrived in the Qalat area, about the same time as Balochi speaking tribes from west; who formed a large kingdom in the 15th century, which soon declined … the whole region falling to the Mughals, descendants of the Mongols, converted to Islam. The Khanate was dominant from the 17th century onwards: till the advent of the British, in 19th century. The signed Treaty of 1876, made Qalat an integral part of the British Empire.

At British withdrawal, in 1948, Qalat became a part of **Pakistan** … In 1955, formally removed from power, the last Khanate of Qalat, is still now, claimed by some of its present-day descendants.

pexels-photo-5303058.jpeg … pexels-photo-6182219.jpeg … pexels-photo-5417955.jpeg … pexels-photo-6018532.jpeg

2. Sibi : **Baluchistan** "**Disenchantment**"! (10 years - 1951 Dec.)

2. Sibi : **Baluchistan** **"Disenchantment"!** (**10 years** - 1951 Dec.)

Sat **he**

in his room alone. He had **abandoned** all jovial **Pleasures** and shunned all gay company, ever but so recluse: always in his reminiscent moods: for his heart suffered much. He remembered the joys he had forgot following a Fatal evening, when he had parted from his beLovéd. Since then, many women luring him into a **dark** corner had murmured **False** accents of **Love**: the smell of female flesh had drown him near, but it's nearness repugnated him,, for in his heart pinched a *Painful* **M**emory of a sweet person,, and he had hastily escaped. But found shelter **Nowhere**; because the only safe escape is to the most **dark** and dreamy sphere of Death: *and Death, the drowsiest of all drowsy* sleeps *... just embosomed him not!*

Thus thought **he**

gloomed and in discord, for he stood torn asunder in a **World** shorn naked,, soothed by 'n of the stunning balming Magic of **Love**.

Restless **he**

paced; he paced a thousand steps, then went quickly quietly out,, shutting firmly the door.

Outside **he**

beheld a **H**aven. A **S**hadowy **Night** permeated all unwieldy objects of a day,, an un-**Earthy** **Beauty** **glowed**. It had drizzled very very **light** and dots of rain had **specked** the whole panorama around. The moon arose 'n sprinkled the **Earth** with strands of **Shimmering** **silver** and the **Complete** scene was ribbed with slight tones of **LIGHT** and **SHADE**. The unwinding road lay a-glinting a strip of **ebony**, where **sombre** **Reflections** gleamed dimly: and the spray-wetted Trees sketched by the sides attempting in vain to form a canopy,, their slender Boughs bloomed with **Night**–green **leaves**; on the rain–**speckled** foliage the countless **specks** ***S**parkled* as the twinkling of dews ... 'twas a dreamy vista of blissful sleep! A cool **W**ind sighed, **leaves** rustled feebly in echoing cadences and drops of **Water** dripped as the **S**harp plucked strings of a **lonely** **lone** **lute**. It was the **H**eavenly Music of the still lofty softy dreaming **Night**! Soft, slow, mellow strains in **Peace** 'n **Harmony** flowed through the **Universe** and **Shivered** through his so **lonesome** a fragile frame.

Around him **he** saw beatific **Nature** lay, as he walked 'n walked and thought of his **L**ove,, and he felt a *Pain* prickling deeply into his insides! And he remembered a similar **Night** years back, when was he a mirthful man,, and had strolled, on 'n on, alike roads. The abiding quiet had been pierced by a hum of tires,, a car had swished ahead and grinded to a stop: a Melodious voice of bells tinkling had invited him in. It was the girl he amoured!

She drove,, **he** dreamt. And suddenly, '**T**ime' did sweep 'n creep 'n sweep; he gazed and drank deep! And lots 'n lots of objects blurring past did peep: and unheeded, went off to sleep.

Met had **he** her at a party and as young men often do, had instantly fallen deeply for her; but she having **N**o**thing** better to fare, had faired and flirted along, as young ladies also usually often do. Days had frolicked 'n frolicked past; he was devoted and happy and she **L**ively and prankish. **S**o**metimes** they disputed over light and much trifling matters,, but later Smiled at their foolishnesses and kissed and patched up their **pretty** petty quarrels,, so that later her chiming **L**aughter filled the air with brimming jollity. Many a **T**imes he took her out and they passed precious moments together. So rident months go by,, for she really had grown to like him, in her own rather special way.

And then **he** was upset. ***J**ealousy* stalked pryingly into their gleeful existence,, for they could not bear the long **lonely** ***H**ours* of separation and out of excessive **E**motion for each other believed the injustices rumoured around. He suspected her of being unfaithful; and she him: and both for no reason but their immense **Love**, which builds an **Edifice** of grievances on no **F**oundations, disbelieved the perfectly simple explanations as signs of faithlessness. They knit Fancy to **burning** facts,, so little Fears loomed large and they looked askance, so un-trustful of each other. Thus they had parted and two **Pearly Tears** had glistened in her downcast **e**yes: what she passing by had flittered with before but held dearest now, had brushed her rudely away! *And in the last moments of togetherness they felt the **R**egret of a **P**ain-staking gain **L**ost.* Then they both were **alone**.

Love be it for **he** or **she**, is an inward glow kindled by shyly shyful Smiles and heart–felt sighs„ a hastened hasty kiss 'n misty eyes; but to lose a **Love** leaves a gaping void which brings sad Memories at the gayest Time. It is as heart renting as to the lonely traveller a Vision, a mirage„ which though pleasing to behold swells up the feeling of emptiness within; as drops of Water, *here there everywhere„ but* ***Nowhere*** *to brim:* of things too dear, but too distant unclear 'n trim!

A dull *Ache*, **he** felt arose in his heart! It was a *Pang* describable not in **W**ords„ nay, un-describable at all: *a falling feeling felt by Lost* ***Lovers*** ***alone!***

Past **Reflections** past **he** gazed vacantly around„ and he thought of his room. So slowly returned **he**.

A fragrant breeze sensed **he** that caressed **Lightly** his **c**heek„ but entered he his room and firmly he re-closed his door.

What **Thought** **he**?

That a Ripening ***L****ife is Wasted through a Jilted* ***Love****!*

What *Concluded* **he**?

That when the ***leaves*** *fall, they fly and scatter blown before an uncertain* ***W****ind„* as is a **Human Soul** scattered and Wasted when the blistering **b**ody is thrown into the boiling **W**arm 'n cold cauldron of **L**ife: '**L**ife', the '*Passion*' on whose '**Entrance**' is 'enGraved' ...

"Disenchantment"!

As a Magician weaves Magic **Charms** un-hung, ... He **He**
Chanting enchanting **W**ords of a færy tongue„ ... Hii Hii
So passing **T**imes a healing potion pour, ... Ha Ha
O'er gaping **W**ounds blown by the scythe of **L**ife; ... He **He**
A few are cured„ as others rot or writhe or soar, ... He **He**
Weeping creeping so end their **lonesome** weary strife: ... Hii Hii
Thus unconcerned, the **Universe** revolves and **rolls** on„ **... Ha Ha**
But ever ...! For ever ...! And ever ...! However ...! In NoN ...... He **He**

Life is a 'Tar' with a 'hick' (Tar'iq) ... Hii Hii Ha Ha (Ha Ha Ha'meed)

Who is Nobody ?

This is a Theme which has haunted me over decades.

Who am I or We or just Us or All of Us.

My first attempt was at 11 years ...

Mr. NOBODY Quetta : **Baluchistan** 1952 Jun.

Then for years, I read and I read and read. Who **Nobody** was?

An effaced person, whose original 'picture', or let us say exactly 'caricature', I found in Ulysses (Homer): old Greek Literature of about 3000 years away.

*Question: "Is **Somebody** Hurting **U**?"* *Answer: "**Nobody**".*

Efforting **Nobody** became **Somebody** ... thus **Nobody** was Not seen, but was Not unheard. Even in the **UnTrue**, existed a '**Nobody**' who was born to become a '**Person**': "**Personne**" in French is "**Nobody**" ... Lost in the green **blue Waves**!!!

My second attempt was at 40 years ...

They say '**L**ife begins at Forty'! Is this Maturity? And out came '**Personne**' ... in Roma in 1981. I spoke No Italian then ... So Why did so many **Nobodys** surrounding surround me? And why did so many **Nobodys** spake so much, that their speech was absolutely **Un-Understandable**?

My third and final attempt was at over half a century old.

But it was only a recapitulation, a translation of all that had been revealed before ... just a plain Translation in English: but very interesting ...

*Because in these all 60 years ... **Nobody** Never Grew Up?*

3. Quetta : **Baluchistan** **MR. NOBODY!** (**11 years** - 1952 Jun.)

Often in the streets

I saw him passing passively by, flitting in and out of the babbling crowd. A vacant stare resided always on his face. In rare moments his common **f**eatures lit up as if by an electric **glow** and he seemed vaguely to realise that he existed very vaguely; but to what end, he never fretted himself with: he had more weighty matters on his **Mind**; such as the price of onions and getting worn sheets repaired at home„ and in office balance–sheets prepared. His **Mind** was a synonym to a big blank vaguely, and of reason he was only 'n very scant; but scantier still was of **L**ive **E**motions: **a barren rut in a scorched heath is more fertile**.

Ô! Such was

The Mr. Nobody: **Nobody of This World, I knew**.

Once as 'twas

that I had asked him about what he **thought** of **L**ife 'n whether it's better to end an uncreative, unoriginal existence or to **L**ive on unproductively, unremembered for havin' **? what ?" ...** a complicated reply came; then all was sponged from his **Brain**„ for he began prattling about this 'n that, done **Nothing** at all, or had achieved **Nothing** at all? **...**

"? ‹ Ah! › ! ‹ Hm ... ...! › and so and so and blah and blahs;

he started quoting on the subject of ‹'News-Papers and'› and "Money and" and "'**World** Market' and 'Domination beyond Manipulating the Common Wealth and'". Secret Fears him assailed„ suddenly relapsing to an afflicted **S**ilence; grieved over the possibility of cockroaches breeding in his pantry: and half-apologetically half-apprehensiously, he hurried away to look further into this dire contingency.

One day as

he sat **alone**, he let his **Mind** wander and it led him to a half-remembered land of greenery where one spends his lisping–age. Day long, with his companions, he scrambled about in bushes„ **experiencing** a naïve joy in everything. But as he grew older, the glory of those days had faded; child-hood ties were ***Broken*** and what he held nearest his heart was estranged: **passage through** Spring **to** Autumn **reaches** **yellower** regions„ 'twas an oldish man now, 'n his family unit was almost reduced to **nil**. His Narcissism clashed him with **Humanity** and liberty and never did his **L**ife mellow nor did he seek Devine purpose in it; a dreary material **World** pressed down and leaving aside **Ideals**, he soon settled into a smuggy cheerless rut„ and honoured going back on his **W**ord of mouth„ for convenience or commercial sense. Thus, **Profit forgets Promise**: so he kept on traversing from bleaker to more arid 'n jejune zones. To espouse finance to be found anywhere, even **Human Love** is weighed; ***in a sterling of a pound***. He might have felt a strong **Revulsion** at his mechanical existence„ but now being well accustomed to it, thus forgot that there is **Something** higher in **L**ife„ a **Something** much higher in this **L**ife, than only **L**iving it itself!

Oft so„ so is

that thoroughly indoctrinated, as are so many politicians of their own self-righteousness, he went about his mischievous business washing from his **Brain**, all **thoughts** of realisation„ or any honest or silly points of view. And I saw him pressing by in the street but never was sure if it was the same person I had seen before„ for he had a whole brood of friends and relations and all were exact replicas of each other: all engaged in negotiations, regarding the so important '**talks about talks**'„ about **talks about talks**„ about talking 'n talking talks.

Over days past at last, news

reached me that he Died; he had passed away quietly, lamented by a few and remembered only by very little or even less or lesser. So our Mr. **No**body left to **No**body, what he had or had not … very little or even much less or lesser … In a few years also the signs of his Grave were obliterated. Thus he who **L**ives for mere wealth or power, at the end of a hypocritical existence is swept away from men's **M**emories, as is a small rainless **cloud** blown o'er along **Infinte** expanses of **H**eavens to **UnenLightened** regions obscure.

Only truth is„

that this had really been the short-statured Mr. **No**body I had known. I'm told he left his last phase to a foolish brother **Somewhere** in the West. I think it was him, for his visage **Waves** 'n wavers so very hazy before my **e**yes, that I Doubt if it all is not just a figment of my own imagination got, which with a little lapse of **T**ime, will be **burnt buried** 'n **battered**!

P.S. : I learned later in **L**ife, what Dr. Johnson had said about 'Will Shakes' … casting a Doubtful Light on 'Bill', as far as learning or knowledge was concerned …

'Knowing **Little Latin and Less Greek**'

So our **No**body evolved Slowly … From One to **Nothing** … Unto One unto **Something** …

Lacking NoN-Words unto Words … Finally … A Better Me …

N O B O D Y ... ... (Lörrach : 1993) ... See me in NoBody ...

There are **people** who just **come** head
'n there are people who **just do go**:
'n in this **hustle-bustle** of **com-in' 'n go-out'**,
destiny created **a solitary** being ... **who**
from want of **another** denomination
was called **N**o**body**.
Why **so** so **so** so silk,
That he understood **not**,
he had asked **never** for **anything**.
Somehow he arrived; 'n thus **was it**.
Then he started to live **alone** very **quietly**
'n people started knowing him rather **vaguely**.
He was AMONG the others ... but **not OF the others**.
And **so** a voice **startling** started to run between his **friends** :
"**Somebody like N**o**body**, there is **n**o**body** other **in this World** !"
This he had heard many times by so many people **since his infancy**,
but it did not impression him any ... he wanted to be simple like **Everybody**.
Everyone said he **was different** from the others„ **without understanding** the **Why**,
but 'he knew the **why of whys**'„ 'cause **Destiny** had **never hidden** her **designs from him**:
he was not at all of this world ! "**The Ordinary is not in me**": is the **toughest** of all **knowledge**. belly

Many **people** to **be-come**
'n many people to **be**-**gone**:
'n they are all **forgotten forlorn**.
So centuries have **passed 'n rolled**
'n still one speaks always of our **N**o**body**,
a no-**one** small presence with an **invisible face**
who often had felt the **pains of** very **sensitive beings**.
One says often among those„ going a-past bide **beyond time**,
"**N**o**body** cannot be understood, **he has a none being,**
"he is only **a thought** 'n his **equal hasn't been**
"Anywhere **Anybody**„ never **in this world**".
'Twas the only gift that **Destiny** had **reserved** ever **thus for him**„
but he paid it very dear : **in an eternity** of solitude in **a crowd so void of people** ...
'n what so **funny** is, he had **never** even **asked** of **anybody** for **anything**„ **ever or when**, when **???** feet

... many people to gather & speak in an opera to-gether ... so the moving finger WRITEs ... in a 2nd session ... read only **full words in 'bolds'...**

(*Free Translation from an earlier version„ a final end* ***sound*** *rime in the* ***1st. letter*** *of alphabet„* ***'a' at last***)

P E R S O N N E ... ... (Roma : 1981) Nobody (Lörrach : 1993) ...

testa

Les gens viennent et les gens partent. Dans ce **va et viens éternel**, destin créa
un être que par **manque d'autres** dénominations on nomma **Personne**. Pourquoi si **en soie**,
personne ne comprit; **Personne** n'avait rien demandé. Enfin il arriva **là**,
terra ferma, et voilà ! Puis les gens l'ont connu vaguement car il commença **à**
vivre; simplement "vivant parmi les **autres**, il n'était pas des **autres**": et vibrant la
douleur des **autres**, il n'était point des **autres**; ainsi une rumeur a couru, "Il n'y a **pas**
d'autres Personne dans ce monde" ! Depuis l'enfance il l'a entendu maintes fois, cela ne l'**a**
guère impressionné. **Personne n'était simple**, comme tout le monde; un t**as**
de gens disait qu'il était **différent sans savoir**, mais lui sut pourqu**oi**,
parce que le **destin ne lui cacha jamais ses desseins** : il n'était pas de ce monde, sa cr**oix**!

pancha

*"L'ordinaire n'existe point en **moi**"*

est la plus dure des connaissances de **soi** ... il diamante dell**a** purezz**a** uman**a**!
Des milliers de gens étaient **venus** et sont déjà **parties** : et tous, on les oublier**a**.
Des siècles après ont sombré mais on se rappelle toujours de ce si simple **Personne à**
un visage troublé, cette petite présence **invisible** omniprésente mais effacée, sentant l**a**
peine d'être sensible et souvent parmi ces braves gens le dépassant dans le temps, **ci et là**
on entend, "Solitaire **Personne** ne **s'explique pas**; l'être est une pensée d'au-del**à**, **sois**:
et son égal n'est jamais né et **jamais ne naitra** dans ce monde retourné, d'ici b**as** !"
Destin le farceur, lui a réservé ce seul **cadeau d'immortalité**; cadeau qu'il pay**a**
bien cher: **éternité de solitude** d'une **proche foule pleine de lointains gens** flagad**a**,

piedi pourtant sincèrement, **jamais** il n'a **rien** demandé **à personne** ... ou à qui qu'il **soit** ???

... gens ensemble en un opéra parlent, si en-semble ... ainsi le doigt bougeant ÉCRIT et CRIS... en 2ème. temps ... ne lire que de **mots complets gras** ...

La **1ère.** lettre de l'alphabet est **'a'** ...

... ici le **dernier** son de chaque ligne est en **'a'** ... **a, à, oie, as, oi, oix, ois, oit ...**

4. Quetta : **Baluchistan** **LIMERICKS by LEMUR** (**12 years** – 1953 Jul.)

(i) Once lived a decrepit knight very brave and young
with **dark** **Hair**, green and strong
and a curling moustache, twenty gallant feet long;
He met and courted a lady demure
who Smiled and flashed at him her teeth
all thirty-two or more.
And they would have lived happy after-wards:
God bless them both!
Had not
all his moustache been to the **right**;
and all of her teeth to the **left**.

* * * * * *

(ii) A **C**areless **C**ock from **C**ork **C**alled **C**ook was **C**aught
in a **C**liché in a **C**liff.
They pulled and they pulled and he ne'er came thru;
-do- -do- -do- -do- -do- so he was split in two:
They found out some glue and they stuck him up too,
but, O **miserable** stiff!
They pasted the **beak**-half **back**, hi hi,
and the back-half front.

Limerick : A funny rhyme, often in four parts …

- A Nursery-rhyme has it's Logic … in **Sense**;
- A Limerick has it's Logic … in a **non**-sense:

Thus it keeps on inverting its own reason.

A Critical Study of Some Nursery Rhymes ... A Fine Corollary (2003)

A Nursery Rhyme is a traditional poem or song for children in Britain and other countries, but usage only dates from the late 18th / 19th century. In North America the term Mother Goose Rhymes, introduced in the mid-18th century, is often used.

The Secret History of the Nursery Rhyme ... Many of the origins of the humble nursery rhyme are believed to be associated with, or reflect, **actual events in history**! Also there exist often ... **concepts of political domination** ???

Nursery Rhyme	Critical Words	Objective
Goosy goosy gander, where shall I wander; Upstairs and downstairs, in my lady's chamber; There I met an **old man** who wouldn't say his **prayers**; I took him by the left leg and threw him **down the stairs** !	old man **wouldn't say his prayers** took him by the left leg **threw** him down the stairs	**Children are taught Religious Ferocity**
Humpty Dumpty sat on a wall, Humpty Dumpty had a big fall; And all the King's horses, and all the King's men, Couldn't put Humpty **Dumpty** together again !	**H**umpty **D**umpty **King**'s horses **King**'s men Couldn't put together	**Ridiculous Commoner ? Superiority of Royalty ?**
Rain rain go away, come back another day; Little Johnny wants to play, rain rain go away; Rain rain go to **Spain**; Do **not show** your face again !	Rain rain go away (Spanish **Armada**) not show your face again (Queen **Elisabeth** First)	**"God blew His winds, and England was saved !"**
Three blind mice ... (repeat) : See how they run ... (repeat); They all went after the farmer's wife who cut off their tails, with a carving knife; *Did you ever see* such a sight in your life ? (**3 blind mice**) !	Three **blind** mice (repeats) **cut** off their **tails** with a **carving knife** *see* **such a sight** ?	**A laughing matter !!! Cruelty on Infirmity ?**
Eeny meny mayna mo, (play) Catch a nigger, by his toe; (force) If he screams, let him go; (torture) Eeny meny mayna mo ! (amusement)	child counts **nigger**, **toe** **screams**, let him go *spin around head & throw*	**Children are taught Racial Violence**

Funnily, an amusing matter ... Self-Justified!!! hi hi ...

J'ai dit bizzare bizzare ... comme c'est bizzare ? (Dr. Knock)

So have you understood ??? Do you understand ???

What is Civilised 'n What is so Un... 'n What's Hypocrisy ... Aaaamen ?

There is nothing either good or bad, but thinking makes it so ...

Colloquy to dear Horatio ... (Hamlet ... Shakespeare)

History is Written by the Conqueror ... is **Truth in False-hood** (2021)

A lil bit about ... English Literature ...

1. Francis **Bacon**: the Aristocrat ... (22/1/1561 - 9/4/1626) ...
   Bacon's Cipher ... Advocate of Scientific Knowledge & Exposition, on a base of Inductive Reasoning, by an Argumentative Approach; Sceptically & Methodologically Observing Mother Nature's Order ... Scientific Inquiry, produced ... **The New Atlantis**; History of **Life & Death**; **Wisdom of Ancients**.

2. William **Shakespeare** (Sheikh Peer) ... (26/4/1554 - 23/4/1616)
   4 last plays made **William**, a Shakespeare ... **Hamlet**, **Lear**, **Macbeth**, **Tempest**: "There is method in his madness": "Who is it that can tell me who I am?": "If it were done when 'tis done, then 'twere well It were done quickly": "Misery acquaints a man with strange bedfellows" ... He was the only writer in the world, who used a fabulous vocabulary ... an Incredible **23000 words**; as **ill**, as **well**.

3. John **Milton**: the **Blind** Poët ... (9/12/1608 - 8/11/1674) ...
   Paradise Lost ... **Lucifer**: "Better to Reign in Hell, than Serve in Heaven" ... Normal Vocabulary is 300 words; bit Educated is 600; Average Writer is 900; Better Writer 1200; Good Writer 2500 ... but Milton employed **5000** words, Coining New Words from Latin & Greek: Used blank verse; No Rimes.

4. Dr. Samuel **Johnson**: ... (18/9/1709 - 13/13/1784) ...
   Adamant Criticiser of Shakespeare: his famous phrase ... He **Knew little Latin and Less Greek** ... Critic Renowned, but at times biased! Gained 1500 guineas: **Dictionary of the English Language**.

5. Famous Lines of Famous Poëts: that **Changed the History** of English Language ...
   1. "Was this the **face** that launched a thousand ships" ... Thomas Marlow (Dr. Faustus: **Helen**)
   2. "To be **or not** to **be**, that is the question" ... Shakespeare (Hamlet: simply, **Boolean** Maths.)
   3. "**Beauty** is **truth**, **truth beauty**; that's all ye know and all ye need to know" ... John Keats
   4. "*Drank coffee and sat for an hour*" ... T.S. Eliot (Wasteland: **Spoil** of 2000 years Construct?)
   5. "**Thanks**, I am a Vegetarian" ... Bernard Shaw (Comment: when one admired a **Lady's Legs**?)
   6. "**Eloquent Silences**" ... Samuel Becket (Waiting for Godot): Harold Pinter (The Dumb Waiter)

A lil bit about ... English History ...

1. Elisabeth the 1st. ... **The Slave Trade** ... She enjoyed its Profits; also African Entertainers in Court: by her approval, Captain John Hawkins, captured 300 Africans in 1562; which he traded against hides, sugar & ginger. Again in 1564, an expedition had Elizabeth's benediction, with a ship.'Twas strange, that an **African** Slave, in later dates, cost £50, while an **Irish** was Cheap? Only £5/-! To Throne, Charles Stuart in 1660, realised that Slaves were as profitable as Sugar Plantations? And established was, The Royal Africa Co. (RAC), supplying Slaves to British West Indies? **'Tis History**! Politicians & Notables United, provided slaves for French West Indian Colonies, making Fortunes! During **British Irish Rule**, "**Indentured Servants**", were subjected to **Forced Labour** in America!

2. Queen Victoria ... Chinese today, name the 19th. Century, as the "Century of Humiliation". **Reason**?
   1. 1st. Opium War (1839-1842) ... Warring, Qing & Britain: triggered by illegally dumping over 300 Opium Tons year, by the British Naval Ships? **The battle was Lost by the Chinese**.
   2. 2nd. Opium War (1856-1860) ... Warring, Qing & British & French: military and naval force superiority of the allies, could have only one result! **The battle was Lost by the Chinese**.
   3. 1st. & 2nd. Convention of Beijing ... Kowloon Cession & South of Shenzhen River & Lantau.

3. Elisabeth the 2nd. ... Modern English Society has suddenly realised, that "**Money Whitening**" has become a really serious problem. Brunt is often practiced by known **Corrupt Politicians** (Indo-Pak) Base. What Future will hold, is Unknown: but is surely creating a Racial Upper Cast Anomaly ... Present Government suffers serious Criticism: that this **Pseudo-Political Protection** be eliminated!

What's said? **Facts** Not **Fantasy** ... **Traditions** Respect **Traditions** ... *No Tradition is Superior*: only, **Time-Bound**!

... Slaves' Coins **Glitter** in **Darkness** ... **Golds Glitter** in **Bank**s ... **Stars Glitter** in the **Sky** ...

5. Lahore: Punjab **Adolescence** (13 years – 1954 Apr.)

ttps://www.pexels.com/search/balochistan%20Pakistan/ ... pexels-photo-4610272.jpeg ... pexels-photo-2383832.jpeg ... ... pexels-photo-2240891.jpeg ... pexels-photo-2734406.jpeg ...

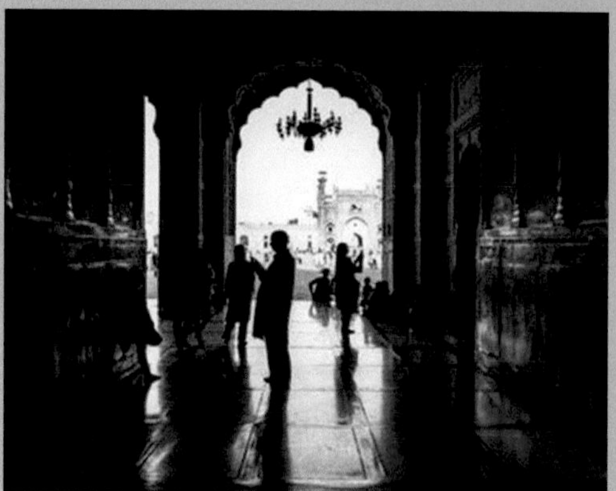

Gates of Lahore; Roshnai Gate. "Roshnai Gate," (the "Gate of Lights"), is located between the Lahore Fort and Badshahi Mosque. In the evenings, the gate was lit up, hence its name. It is the only gate that is in good condition and still retains its original looks.

Lahore, popular City of Gardens and Colleges, the second largest city of **Pakistan**, and the capital of **Punjab**. The cultural heart of **Pakistan** and hosts most of the many arts, festivals, film-making, music: and intelligentsia of the country.

As far back as 4000 years ago, some historians trace the history of this famous city. However, its proved that **Lahore** is at least 2,000 years old, dating to Alexander the Great and **Porus**, the Punjab King. Hieun-tsang, famous Chinese pilgrim, gives a vivid description of **Lahore**,when visited in early 7th century AD ... From 1524 to 1752, **Lahore** was the Mughal Empire: later becoming a province of the Afghan Empire. Then ruled Sikhs, from 1799 to 1849: annexed by **British Raj**, 1849 until 1947 (**Independence**).

... pexels-photo-127753.jpeg : Lake Siaf ul Malook ... Siaf ul malook-05.jpg (Myself :Own Photo) ...

5. Lahore : Punjab **Adolescence** (**13 years** – 1954 Apr.)

(As if Reading from a Text)

Middle-Agéd Man : The **Reflection** of Autumn in the mossy-hued Water: when the bare branches garbed in Wintery solemnity stipple the slow uneven Water which ripples it's different **Shades** of disturbed velvet on to the other **Shore** clustering to ***Brokeness***. And deep below the daubs of clouds move, till from a **Lighter** patch an invisible **Ray** dips down, to brighten an occasional group of playful **Waves** whose surfaces glint like isolated points of **Steel** exhilarating in their irregular dance of irregular **Rhythms**,, all so well co-ordinated: and thus the clouds keep passing so **S**ilent and variant in their monotony. Then a dry **leaf** is swept in and races alongside a small boat, past a half-merged **R**eed over a full submerged **R**ock, across a **muddy** furrow; till the child runs to the other edge of the **Pond** and diverts the boat to another course. And there in the pleasantly nipping **W**ind stands a **lonely** old man **experiencing** the evanescent moment existing individually until it is swallowed away in the harsh **L**ife composed of un-**Natural** sounds. And the solitary child plays on by the edge of the **Pond**, oblivious of the roar and tumult created by **Humanity** in its haste to escape the thousand indiscriminating claws of **Blind D**estiny who creates infinite flaws in **enacting** it's discordant opera of figures 'n indexes that we call men: and so scattering a few tragic corpses here 'n anew corpses there, never ever says another **W**ord about the millions of sincere men who are defeated in their most earnest **Ideals**.

And he watched the innocent child play with his **P**aper-boat: till the patient and **S**ilent old man, old as the **C**aves in whose closed depths even the far echoes return rasping and freckled, was led into a strange irrational **World**; where above the Autumn air appeared to the child's **e**ye a snow-capped **Sky** of melting icicles clothed in fine **pretty** dresses of ***Fire***: where the Water-drops falling are changed to beads of glass,, and in the low spreading **brown** hazy **Shimmer** more **pretty** than the **Lustre** of ripples under moon-lit **Nights** of a færy-land.

'Twas there that walking beside a Phantom **Lake**,, he asked a hundred simple questions, when the **W**ind breathed upon the bathéd Trees and made them shake off their stupor.

“ Grampa ! Why do the **leaves** move ? ”

“ The **W**ind makes them move ! ”

“ How does it make them move ? ”

“ By moving itself ! ”

“ But why does it move itself, grampa ? ”

“ Because you can't expect it to stand still all the **T**ime, can you ! ”

“ No, I suppose not. Aren't you awfully clever to know all that ?

Thus tell me now ... How old are you, grampa ? ”

“ Seventy-seven ! ”

“ Golly, you are big. And I am only six. Just three **T**imes and a half as big as I am !

Grampa ? **Do you believe in færies** ? ”

“ No ! ”

“ Were you ever a child once, grampa ? ”

“ Yes ! ”

“ Did you ever believe in **færies** then ? ”

“ Yes ! ”

“ Then why don't you believe in them now ? ”

“ Because I've grown ever so old now ! ”

“ You mean **færies never grow old** ? ”

“ No ! ”

“Oh. Wouldn't you like to be a **færy** then, grampa ?

Then you'd never grow old, and never have to cut your beard every day !

Would I also be grown-up once ? ”

“ Yes ! ”

“ And have a beard too ? ”

“ Yes ! ”

“ Where will you then be ? ”

“ Resting I suppose ! ”

“ Why ! Would you be very tired ? ”

“ I think so ! ”

“ And you'd be cutting your beard everyday still ? ”

“ No. That would be resting too ! ”

“ Oh ! It would also be very tried ? ”

“ Yes ! ”

“ And when I grow old, will I be very tired and rest too ? ”

“ Yes ! ”

“ Where will I rest, grampa ? ”

“ **Somewhere** ... **Here** or **There** ! ”

" Oh, wouldn't that be nice ! But why will I grow tired ? "

" Don't you feel tired at the end of each day and so sleep at **Night**fall ! "

" Yes. Why do I ? "

" Well, after lots and lots of years when all work is done, you will lie down to rest,, to rest again, and then go off to sleep. Only that 'sleep' is called 'Death' and lasts all the **T**ime that you are waiting or awaiting or awake, or that you are asleep ! "

" **What** is this 'Death', **grampa** ? "

"Death's **the story which ends all stories** !

The endless beginning of all ends and all **T**imes: of all ***Broken*** **Hopes**: of **Hop**eless patience ! The **R**emembrance which is forever forgotten: and comes only to people the imagination with beings who never materialise and remain as elusive and unreal as we ourselves will be, to remain in the **M**emory of a **Loved** one ! "

" Does that mean that I can rest, now if I want to ? "

" **Hush** ! Do you see that Bird **There** ? "

" No ! **Where** ? "

" Upon that thick Tree **Here** ... out **There** ? "

" No. But I think I can hear it sing. Grampa ! Have you ever seen a cuckoo ? "

" Yes ! "

" The Bird that comes out of a cuckoo–clock and says 'cuckoo-cuckoo' ? "

" Yes ! "

" **What** is it made of ? "

" Of wood ! "

" But **How** can it sing if it is made of wood ?

" So justly tell me ? **How** can a Bird sing, if it's made of pure wood ?

"Grampa ! **Don't tell me you are lying** ? "

" No, my child ! "

" But don't so many grown-up people lie ? "

" Yes, they do ! "

" **Why** do they lie ? "

" I think they just have to ! "

“ **Will I also lie When I am grown–up**, grampa ? ”

“ I suppose so ! ”

“ **Then** will I be punished for lying ? ”

“ Not if you feel sorry for it and never ***Harm*** anyone ! ”

“ How many people have you ***Harmed***, grampa ? ”

“ I don’t know. Many perhaps ! ”

“ And so many must have ***Harmed*** you to-o ? ”

“ I guess so ! ”

“ Grampa? **Why do people** ***Harm*** **each other** ? ”

“ *Because there are so many and they want so much*

that some have to get ***Hurt***„ once in a while ! ”

“ **And Where do all the people go When they have been** ***Hurt*** ? ”

“***Nowhere****! Just keep on* ***L****iving as everybody else does, I suppose !* ”

“ **But Where do all these people come from** ? ”

“ *From a land of* ***Ængels*** *where all is sweetness !* ”

“ **Then Why do they come Here** ? ”

“ *Because they are to-o greedy and selfish to* ***L****ive like the* ***Ængels*** *!* ”

“ **I thought you didn’t believe in færies** ? ” “ I don’t ! ”

“ **But aren’t Ængels like large færies** ? ”

“ *Only one* ***L****ives in a child’s* ***Mind****„ the other in the adult’s !* ”

“ **What's the difference, between a child and an adult**, grampa ? ”

“ *A child has a better chance to become an* ***Ængel****, but an adult often not:*

he is much to-o much occupied in this **Worldly World** ! ”

“ **Grampa ? How does one become an Ængel** ? ”

“ *Be like they go-od* ***mother*** *when she walked ’pon this* ***Earth*** *!* ”

Youth : He remembered his **mother** not: but he did remember a gypsy **maiden**, who stole from the **Stars** the twinkle in her **e**ye and *thus gay in her innocence surpassed the gaiety with which **Nature** kisses the **c**heek of the **flower** and the child.* She **L**ived and sang upon the **Shore** of a quiet **Lake**. Pure and simple, a **RA NBOW** over the **Lake** suffused the evening air with **Poetry** and **Art** and **Creation**: that every single hushed movement breathed of ¶usc; 'n seemed to ask if ever there was an arc more perfect than that of the fine **RA NBOW** which loops the **Sky** in its mute splendour! Born of and pitted against the **S**ilent glory of the **Sun**, patiently it bides its vacant ***Hour*** ... a myth to the naïve child„ a revelation to the weary philosopher ... and then retires to its **n**ether home. And it's outer **S**hadow lingers a misty moment more„ more **Beautiful** than itself but unobserved and neglected in an atmosphere spontaneous in it's **Magic**. And then the **Sun** is set and the **Stars** ridicule that ever there existed anything which surpassed them in the aloof **Beauty**, of ¶ystery and grandeur!

Girl : Thus he wooed her! That she cared not for him„ he held not against her: but that he **Loved** her a little too much„ bore him **L**oneliness and **W**isdom! And when last he saw of her„ she danced lithely to the tunes of a **banjo**: and many a many **violin** !

" **That Night fell I in Love** " ... said grampa.

Woman : The circle of a child's **World** is **Complete** to be diversified into segregated segments by the ongoing age, till a wrinkled freckled old man is left totally in isolation, in an empty hole ... the whole circle of an entire **Complete Nothing** ... **the Total and Full Nothingness** ...

Mid-Agéd. Man: The **W**him**s**ical child in him **W**rangled up unto the surface; and the monologue resumed again„ like strands of **thoughts** without any singular theme.

" Grampa! **What is Night made of ?** "

" ***Nothing** but **S**hadows and **F**eelings.* "

" **And what is Love made of ?** "

" ***Ôf Nothing**, my child.* "

" **Then what is Nothing made of ?** "

" ***Ôf** Ashes **Ôf Love Ôf L**ife **Ôf** Images **Ôf** Reality.* "

" Grampa! **Do you know the difference between a Dream and a Reality ?** "

" ***A Dream may yet be a Reality once**: <u>but</u> all that's **R**eal slips Past the Barrier of Present 'n Exists only as a Dream 'n **So**m**ething** which Never will Come by 'n Doubtful that it Ever did Before!* "

“ **Then why do we always get a dream when we are asleep and never get a Reality** ?

Grampa, **there**'s an anomaly„ **here** 'n **there** 'n **then** 'n **when** ? ”

“ *Yes. For to get a **R**eality you must be awake!* ”

“ **But if a Reality becomes a dream, why are we never asleep when we are awake** ? ”

“ We think we are not; but that's all that we **L**ive for! The wingéd present seemingly so important in itself corrodes away in the unknown future to a few Visionary glimpses of the dreamy past: a halo of **N**othing but all emptiness ... that's what we consist of! ”

Mid-Agéd. Man : “ For all thy *Pains* thou learnest to know thyself and why thine heart is so Anguished! *For even **Blind D**estiny must have hid some plan in men's mis**F**ortune!* ”

Youth : “ Is it merely a **J**oke that she makes thy **F**eelings of such stuff that can be *Broken*, **burnt**, **crushed**, **abandoned** and dis-regarded and still be as succumbant to *Hurts* as a sapling mango to the frost ? And yet still unrewarded we go, just wanting to **L**ive an unstained existence, satisfied just with a Vision ... a ***Beatrice***, an image: only the surge of bathos wipes out what our ancestors called **R**eality, pretending that our ephemeral existence is in itself a **R**eality„ worth the effort involved to keep it perpetual. ”

Mid-Agéd. Man : “ Thy reason stems from a sense of loss, of Anguish ...

for *thou knowest well how is it to* ***L**ove,* **but** *not how it is to be **L**oved.* ”

Youth : “ Only if the Anguish in thy heart may cast an Eternal *Tear* and make a name **immortal** ... that would be reward enough for one who, like a trail-less **S**tar exits un-applauded, **burning** off, unto 'n from the theatre of the **Universe** ...

And then to wish no more but to be no more! ”

Mid-Agéd. Man : And the old man watched the child, happy that a whiff of a **W**ind carried his boat faster 'n faster across the **Pond**: carried his **L**ife further 'n farther into the pit! And wondered that one day he too will grow up in the city of many locked doors which regularly blinks its **LIGHTS** off 'n on„ 'n on 'n off; 'n off 'n on for each passing day„ 'n then finds that his grand **Idylls** amounted to **N**othing: **N**othing but a **N**othing ...

... **helplessly Suffering the base pollute his God–like images** ...

... Locked out of the terrain over which as ever a whisper steals ...

Maiden : " Pray … *Break* **not my enchantment ever„**

for I am a dreamy **thought** of things only in dreams„

and exist must **alone** in myne 'n thyne dreams„

and were the Dirty fingers of **Earthly** even to touch me„

then lose'ud I my **Eternal Charms„** and crumple to the Filthy Dirty **Earthy** Dust beneath. "

*Afraid, that forever **be made mundane the** Divinity **of all idols„** 'n all imaginations untold.*

Voice of BeLovéd : Pollute NOT the little silken **beach** in the plain **p**alm of **Universe** whose twinkling **P**articles of softly resplendent **sand** were ruffled by their playful **f**ingers„ where sate he by her **R**emembrance and watched the triple moon in her **e**yes, the **Sea** and the **Sky** … and the canopy of **S**tars beside … cast up from the bottom of the **Sea„** to be-stud the **Sky** high above! Dangling lowly … so above …

… Nota …

Surprising … written at 13 … now 2021 (**am about 80**)

- **There** is only **One C**haracter … **T**ime … as … as **Couple**

- **He** … Child, **Adolescent** … **Y**outh, **M**iddle-Agéd, **Grampa**
- **She** … **G**irl, **W**oman … **Maiden**, **V**oice, **B**e**L**ovéd

- **The** One **Unit** Time **Exists** … **Extends** … **V**isible unto an Internal **Mind**.
- **And All That Exists** … **Exists** Simultaneously … **L**iving 'n **L**oo**king„** 'n in **Loving**.

… **TIME ?** … **NO** **P**ast, **P**resent, **F**uture … **O**NLY **Universal** …

6. Lahore: Punjab **A Night in a Lonely Shack** (14 years – 1955 May)

... https://www.pexels.com/search/balochistan%20Pakistan/... pexels-photo-744667.jpeg ... pexels-photo-4035587.jpeg ...
... pexels-photo-4004375.jpeg ... pexels-photo-4298692.jpeg ... pexels-photo-5417957.jpeg ...

... pexels-photo-4043643.jpeg ... pexels-photo-3995673.jpeg ... pexels-photo-5721094.jpeg ...

6. Lahore: Punjab **A Night in a Lonely Shack** (14 years – 1955 May)

6. Lahore : Punjab **A Night in a Lonely Shack** (**14 years** – 1955 May)

Nota 2017: It's the only story written in all my wanderings, where the central character is purely fictional (imaginary),, but I have tried to make it as real as possible; as **L**iving as was possible ...

Nothing happened for a long time !

Then from far arose the heavy rumble of the overhanging clouds; this **lone** broil spread to all **H**eavens and groaned in **P**ea**c**e 'n **H**ar**mo**n**y** with the kiss of **W**inds and the **S**ilence of surroundings. The hovering clouds became **darker** and thicker and the **W**ind blew stronger and colder. The **Night** grew older. View **Somewhere** in the **W**ild **W**ilds**, while a few prayed** then sho-ok their **h**eads,, and **F**earing hearts searched long into the ***black*** ***Nothing*** *of the evening passed:* they lo-oked up to the clouded **f**ace of the mo-on which **seemed like a lady shrouded** ... thus so, **'n dark 'n grey** ... **in dark 'n grey** greaving over the **D**eath of a be**L**ovéd,, to-o stunned to be **C**rying! And then even that wasn't there anymore, no more,, for **blackness** enveloped all **!**

Suddenly **L**igh**tening** cracked. A streak of molten chrome flashed across the **Sky**,, and for a moment all **Universe** lit up, as if the **C**reator chose to pass that way. Then the stunning brilliance plunged into the **blackest** of **darknesses**: *pitchy as mid-**Night** in a **S**torm-tossed **D**erelict **haunted** by nameless **spectres**,,* that not even the **Shi**mm**erings** of a sputtery **Candle** to dilute the fluid **inky** atmosphere **!**

But how? In this **dark**, a **silhouette** moved at a staggery pace,, no refuge offered. The rise and fall of the **G**round swayed before appearing to stretch on to a long **Nothing**ness,, revealing no sign of **Human** habitation. The **S**hadow trudged to the bald top of a rise; 'n in exhaustion sat down on a mound **!**

Thunder muttered to itself and the sound came hollow,, as a resounding **M**acabresque voice of a **D**ead man **predicting do-om from the deep depths of Eternity**! All the forces of **Nature** seemed to compass at a one single point,, awaiting an opportune moment to descend with all its flapping ***Fury*** and leave **D**estruction in its passing wake,, **D**estruction worse than the **D**ebris left by the gonged **F**atal **blows of T**ime **which vanquishes the mightiest and never even pauses to wonder over the futility of** mortals' **efforts,, the uselessness of efforts** ! *Mocking nature **Laughs** at the boast of man who has no power at all,, and whatever he has is but less than **Nothing**:* **all** ***Pain*-fully bent to construct D**estruction! Thc **W**ind developed into a **G**ale and its howl sounded like the tormented **C**ry of a long **L**ost **Soul** in an eerie **W**ilderness **!**

*Then **Blinding** **L**igh**tening** crashed,, and **T**hunder **T**hundered duly* **!**
*The sheeting rain-**S**torm poured obliquely down,, in its do-om-day **F**ury* **!**

In that brief moiety of an **I**llumination, the solitary figure perceived at a distance a **D**eserted shack. It got up, wrapped the cloak tight around itself and proceeded towards it. The rain lashed, the chilling **W**ind bit hard,, and the **C**ol**o**u**r**less form lo-osing it's fo-ot-hold, stumbled often. At this **T**ime it would have even been glad, to seek refuge with the **g**rizzly company of the creatures of the soil, had it been possible to crawl so deep so under-**G**round. With slow steps the stranger reached the shelter, crossed the **R**uinous threshold and opened the creaking do-or cautiously,, *so little by little by little by little* **!**

"Get out !"

Suddenly a tense male voice, as the cracking report of a pistol-shot, rang out and the intruder was jerked to a stop. It was a bare cabin: some straw up-piled on one side and a *Broken*-down cot lay in a corner under which was placed an old chest. A masculine shape sat half-crouched beside a rudely designed *Furnace*, in which a few *Coals* smouldered; waiting their end !

"Please let me in. I got caught out in the rain", implored the daunted feminal voice of the Mysterious wondering wanderer !!

Hearing this, the man jumped up and came closer. He was panting like a person who has been engaged in a short fight. Behind him, a faint rufescent **glow** of the *Embers* made his enlarged wavering **U**mbræ fall on her: she saw his features only as indistinct lines. He offered her his **a**rm and helped her inside. Tired, she lay down on the straw and he hung her wet cloak on a nail. The **S**torming **W**indy **S**torm raged and she **thought** that she heard a noise outside; all other sounds were downed 'n drowned the next instant in a **T**hunder clap. He peeped out, banged the door shut, came and sat down near her !!!

"Are you all right **?**" He asked !!!!

There seemed **Something** familiar about this deep bass voice; but she had known so many men that there always appeared **Something** familiar about all voices !!!!!

She simply replied **...** "Yes. Only just a little wet **!**"

For a short while he contemplated about the indelicacy of asking her to remove her clothes so as to dry them„ but laid aside this solicitation and instead stated, "A woman shouldn't expose herself to such weather at this **T**ime of **Night**, 'n also at such a **lonely** place. It may be Dangerous. You may catch pneumonia 'n Die **!**"

To her **Mind** came the picture of her husband lying Dead; her first thought had been that she would be accused of **Murder** and had run away. On the point of blurting out all her past, she checked herself and clarified not altogether un**Truth**fully !!!!!!

"I was turned out of home **!**"

"But pray, **Why ?**"

"My husband suspected me of infidelity **!**"

"A **True** suspicion **?**" Escaped his **t**ongue **! ! !**

"**Yes**", came a frank reply **! ! !**

Puzzled, he looked at her in **S**ilence; then finally ventured to ask the question which loomed foremost in his **Brain** !!!!!!! "But tell? **Who 'n What you are 'n from Where;** say **?**"

She did not answer directly: f*or troubled* ***Minds*** *find solace only in* **S***ilence ... in the unending and the endless combinations of* **Something** ***Truly*** *meaningless,* **because ...**

meanings gush back thoughts„ which are the Springs of all problems ! ! ! ! ! ! ! !

She **thought** of the Time when she was a tender imaginative girl of fifteen and in a moment of passion had yielded to a paramour who avowing **Love** later betrayed her fully„ and left her with a three-month gone pregnancy. ***Sometimes** frustrated in one, the inborn **E**motions are glued to a second.* In Desperation she married this 'another' who turned out to be just a drunkard, a ruffian, a gambler„ and who treated her most cruelly whenever in bad humour; and beat her when in good **!**

After a few months her child was born. She **Loved** her innocent-eyed baby with all her heart„ and thus five years had passed: the Despair that her husband's moods flung her into, was sweetened when she heard the unTainted **Laughter** of her growing boy **!**

From behind the screen once, as she watched her off-Spring playing in the street, she saw her older **Lover** pass by„ and knowing the playful child to be his, had hugged it tenderly. He came in to ask 'n tell her husband that he wanted to adopt the boy: and her husband had agreed to the proposal„ his great grief being compensated by a good great sum to be paid immediately, in advance **!**

Her blood boiled bitter„ so resolved to **K**ill the **K**id 'fore the **e**yes of the father„ cause an ancient dictum of the '**Rule of R**evenge' is„ that the *one who has destroyed all a **Happiness** of another ... must have his slightest affection trampled on mercilessly.* With a vengeance, she steeled her **Love** to Poison her Little One„ and Cried un-consoled when even in its *Death–sleep* it Smiled most Trustingly at Her: for a Child's Sincerity looks up transparent to this ***World** so **F**alseness-opaqued.* To hide her crime, that **S**tormy **Night** she threw the now still boy's body in the flooded River. From that day, even her last comfort was snatched off 'n away from her **!**

She never saw her seducer again. Her husband watched his prospective and very imaginary wealth evaporate„ and cursed his ill-luck as the cause of the untimely disappearance of his son. Finding none else who he could make the butt of his ***A**nger*, he vented out, his all pent-up ***W**rath* on her; her lissom **b**ody, he bruised **blue** 'n **black**„ 'n gave hardly any money: that she scarce had scrap to eat. Many a **T**imes wished she to Die„ to slip from the precipice of **L**ife where one crawls step by step„ 'n by 'n by 'n *then* ... *then* to creep or crawl no more **!**

Death **comes but once: and that is all**! But ***H**ate* surged within her; she could not bear to think that he triumphed who had ruined her: so she subsisted! It is a rule of the **World** that those who have any talent market it at the highest price they can afford, or obtain: she possessed no talent except young healthy **f**lesh„ and she rented this commodity at the best rates she could manage„ which returns were not very profitable because many more had adopted alike means for existence ends. Her principle became: '**if U Love them Not, U let them find it out Not**'. At first she felt compunctions stabs„ later it only prickled; for it was just a mark-down of honour, of honour into a very pious high sounding morality„ cause **Even** *ÆEngels* **Learn in Adversity, the Simple 'n Humble Art of Servility**„ of heckling one's self for survival. *And those are not many who do not want to **L**ive* **!**

Finally, her conscious lay dormant and her transactions became a daily routine ... an equation of rudimentary business economy **...** where denotes ***factor* X = €ash**. *Tangled in a labyrinth of slender unpredictable strands, one's aims **S**tray away from one's* **Hop**es **!**

Thus hardened, sustained she herself off 'n on, 'n on 'n off, for the next few years and sank to the lowest depths„ *depths to which no gentle-women sink, or at least, profess that they don't.*

Circumstances maim one helpless !

One evening, while she was gone to a town some distant miles away„ with shy glances and meaningful words ... the t○○ls of her trade ... she had entrapped a male who though he was the *proud father of three grown–ups still longed to be provided by the illicit **Pleasures** everyone often Desires, though admits not;* and they had withdrawn to a secluded place. At that same moment, her husband had also secured an appointment to the same dubious purpose with a lady companion. His consort was late and when he saw a couple stealing away, in his **muddled** Brain *Jealousy* arose that the now she 'the new one' was double–crossing him. Frothing at the **m**outh he had rushed in and in an alcoholic rage had shot Dead her partner. *If it is mirrored in another what one lusts for, an indignant Temper is unleashed;* **I** 'n **V** **R**e**F**e**R** 'n **R**e**V**e**R** the so **R**ighteously **R**igorously **R**eligious: so when he discovered that the female was his wife, he ***piously turned purple with*** *Fury*„ and had ordered her never to enter his house again: he cursed loud 'n swore to flay her a**L**ive in crowd. In trying to defend herself she had pushed him off to where he tottered and fell with a thump„ and due to an over-excited weak heart, expired. She was frightened; but as **No**body except the Dead knew that only she had been with them, she escaped unobserved„ and friendless now aimlessly wandered about in the **Night !**

All came in a flash, but divulged she **No**thing. Uncertain, remained she **S**ilent for a little while„ afraid to be revealed, ***for poverty emits its own effluvia***. Then giving a pseudonym to her inquisitor added ... "As to how I am here, I've already told you. But, pray tell me who you are; and also how happen you to be here **?**"

He got up, paced a few steps and told her that he was a well-known surgeon„ who after a long research had discovered a treatment by which he could resuscitate the Dead. Returning from the next town, his vehicle dashed into the River„ over a Dangerously curved embankment; and he nearly drowned. There just being **no**-**o**ne in sight who could help him, he had started walking: in the Hope of reaching home before Sunset. But he was still a long way off when dusk fell and when the **S**torm *Broke* he had Lost his Path; spying this building he had hurried to shelter hither, till morn came **!**

" Yes, that's what happened to me. Lost my way t○○ " ... joined in the woman ... for she clearly perceived that he was a liar„ a full liar: the chest, the *Broken* cot, the red-hot Ashes all testified that **S**ome**b**ody lived here; and moreover ... how could his clothes still be so dry after such a profound drenching in the River in a **S**torm **!**

" And when you entered I was rather alarmed **!** I Feared that in such a **S**torm no honest company could ever come to this dreary place **!** "

Suddenly became she **S**ilent; all her *Painful* **M**emories returned„ and vainly tried she to drive them away: drive away the *Pain* of **Truth**; for while *the **True** is the dole of the low-trodden* as you can't hide an ïota„

hypocrisy's stare is the luxe of circles up-graded, up-stairs !

She listened to the abating rain pattering on the rc-of and **thought** how much it resembled a child's toddling **f**eet. She shc-ok away this **Reflection** and lc-oked around at the dingy rc-om and her cloak hanging on one side, a nail away; a splotchy puddle of **Dirty Water** had been formed on the bricked flc-or: here and there a cleft or lc-osened brick made the surface uneven. The only window was boarded up with termite–eaten wc-od; in the upper two panes, some splintered glass was still visible. By the occasional bolts of **Lightning**, cobwebs could be noticed adorning the rafters: drips of **Water** streaked down from the corners of the leaky ceiling and patches of plaster had fallen from the moss-**Coloured** walls. In the diffuse **LIGHT**, their **Steel–grey** figures could be discerned squatting down; both were sunk in their private ruminations. This so ancient crumbling a cottage, its dampy exhaling atmosphere intruded on their **Minds**„ and they felt these wan presences pulsating. She **Reflected** how much worse had her **L**ife been than even these deteriorating **Ruins**„ which at least had had a much better past to lc-ok back to„ while she had had **Nothing** but a **desolate F**ate **!** Ô so **desolate** a **F**ate **!**

Her **R**emembrances were ***Broken*** when her companion spoke **!**

" Imagine, how glorious this dump of **Ruins** might once have been with so many a happy **Soul** roaming about. Who can say their **Spirits** may even be floating around at this ***H**our*, lamenting that where they had shared their immense **Happiness** be decayed to such a **Waste**. I remember an old man who once lived in this caving **H**ut and tried to repair it ... maybe he still does? **So**metimes I'm afraid that he will imprison me in here„ *as **L**ife shackles one„* till **Death** only severs the fetters !

I detest him: I contempt the odious walls of this **Fearful** den **!** "

By the slight quaver in his voice she guessed that he was trembling„ and surmised that he was a **coward** tc-o. She was disinclined to conversation„ so consequently did not talk tc-o much **!**

An Eternity seemed to pass !

A full 'n fuller Eternity, again seemed to pass !

The rain had stopped„ 'n the clouds were skittering scattering: *violent gusts shed their **Fury** fast.* Outside, standing all mute the shapeless **Spirits** of the **dark**„ **hazy-grey** outlines behind **darkish** outlines, grasped in their **Ghostly** grip all that ventures forth at this Dead ***H**our*. Bats flutter: afar a shrill owl shrieks; a she-wolf moans. **The waning mc-on is hid behind the shredded Clouds !**

This **darkish** environment„ coupled to the **sombre** apprehensions, compressed down on him; he had a **Phobia** of what lay awaiting him outside: and the blanket of helplessness wrapped itself around his **Mind**. From want of **So**mething to say, he dawdled **! ! ! ! ! ! ! !**

"You must be terribly hungry. I'm sorry **!**

I don't have anything on me except some bank-bills **!**

'Tis gossip ... They contain no nourishing calorie **Value !**"

'Twas then that she realized that she was absolutely penniless, without a dot. In her hurry she hadn't brought along anything with her„ and she didn't know how many hazardous days she may have to **f**ace thus: run aGround with no money under her keel. Her last resort remained ... a calling she had now started to loathe. But having no other way there out, she acted accordingly. He struck a match and went nearer, and some low **W**ords passed between them **!**

' O *what* a cruel **World ?**

Thy *neighbour* gives thee **Friendship !**

To *seduce* thy **Wife ! '**

Then amidst the continuous creaking of the crickets he lay down close beside her„ so very thankful that his **lonely** Fears were allayed 'n shared by another. He fondled slowly her heaving up **b**reasts 'n **whispered** undertones in her **e**ar **!**

Suddenly she slapped him **S**harp 'n sprang up. In that moment she had recognized and now despised the very **t**ouch of him. She abhorred her disgustful profession„ which led her to such baseness that her will remain not her own. Be**W**ildered he sat up and asked what the matter was **!**

" You son of a bitch, you are the one who first made a tramp and a whore out of me **!**
I won't let you soil a single **Hair** of me anymore ... I hate you, I hate you, I hate you **!** "

She screamed out loud **!**

" Now let me see which one are you **?** " So he got up **!**

A bat which had flown in from a hidden cranny, **blindly** arcs about in the air„ they hear the moist flapping of its wings and the dull thuds„ when hitting against a wall it flops down onto the Ground; rats scurry to their holes: piercing the still quietness of the **Night**, a screech-owl ho-ots un-**Naturally** loud from a **S**hrivelled **A**rborescence nearby; away a **lone** wolf howls to warn it's mate: and near the do-or, they harken a croaky mumbling„ which swallowed up in the fading swish of a **W**indy blast, is then heard no more, to sound no more **!**

He had lit a match and while squinting at her was holding it raised above his **h**ead. Grotesque **S**hadows played on his pallid **f**ace: the hollows of his **e**yes receded deeper and leered as the malign **e**ye-**s**ockets of a seared **S**kull freshly dug from a Grave! In his **m**ien imaged the wrapping of ***P**assion* which was tightening around his ***P**anicking* senses: he **d**readed some unnamed ***T**error*„ wanted **Human** nearness to drive his squeezing ***A**ffright* away. He advanced in the threatening posture of an insane gorilla and shouted ...

" You rotten slut, I've paid for my **Pleasure** and I'll have it **!**
Even if I must leave you naked **D**ead **!** "

Cowards cow before strength, but strangle the True weak ... *Revenge Needs Power to reAct* **!**

She fancied that footsteps crunched the rubble outside„ and thinking that **Somebody** might be there to save her, shrank towards the door„ but stumbled against an unfitting Stone and fell. Without thinking she picked it up and hurled it against his **h**ead. He groaned and grossed in Wild **Desires** to copulate with her even **L**ifeless **b**ody, slumped down on the floor. The match-box dropped a-scattering and the **Flickering** ***Flame*** was extinguished **!** In the ***Fire***-grate only one smothered ***Coal*** **burned lone**. With a Dying crackle it cast it's dimly **glowing e**ye on them: then with a last sigh, it went dim. It was oblivious to everything ...

♪ Sooty darkness prevailed ♪

She groped about, found the match-cover and swept up a few sticks„ and struck one ♪ He lay fully spattered in blood ♪ He stirred a little; it faintly dawned that **the clutching hand of** Death **the visitor most** ¶¶ysterious **of all**, approached him fast„ and in an agony he raved ♪♪♪♪♪♪♪♪♪♪♪♪

"... no ... No ♪ I don't want to Die ♪ I won't Die ♪ I can make Dead rise, I won't Die" ♪

In a last convulsion he let his **h**ead jerk loosely ♪

His filmy eye-**b**alls **sizzled towards Infinty** ♪

She let the half-**burnt** match-stick fall ♪ Her **k**nees swayed 'n buckled under her and she felt **R**evulsion at herself ♪ **The survival of the fittest callous** ♪ Seared by the distant **G**ale of **D**estiny, like the **W**retched **C**liffs, erring the helpless protesting sailor„ to his untimely rest ♪♪

There remained no hate for him now„ only pity ♪ He had made her suffer for years un-ending, but in a moment on the verge of extinction„ suffered a million **H**opes of **L**ife being **S**hattered ♪ He just **D**ied ... a fully bottled-up mass of seething whirling hot **E**motions„ in countless ages to be ***Cindered*** from ***Charry Scoria*** to be fused in the elements„ imparting to the **G**ale 'n the **S**quall, their **T**emper 'n their ***Fury*** ♪♪♪

Revenge **fulfilled is R**egret **fretted** ♪♪♪♪

She heard a sob behind, so turned and saw the door being pushed wide open ♪ And in came a very oldened man with a **S**orrow-**whitened** beard, carrying a **Smoky Lantern** in his palsied **h**and„ and with **T**ears in his aged 'n blurred **e**yes, said softly to her ♪♪♪♪♪♪♪♪♪♪♪♪♪♪♪♪

" You have killed my son ♪ You couldn't have helped it ♪ He believed that he was a great doctor with powers to restore the Dead ♪ Often in violent fits of **T**emper„ he beat me out of my hovel, as of today; drove me out of here, where I retired with him whenever he became uncontrollable" ♪ Adding mournfully: " He went mad some ten years back, when in a **S**tormy **Night** he brought back a soaking wet **b**ody, of a Dead child so young " ♪♪♪♪♪

The East-**Sky tinged with argent roused the gilded morn** ♪ A **dejected** solitary woman went out, threw off the coins the madman paid„ and towards some distant unknown land, tread away ...

a lone greyish speck framed against the bluing goldish mist-clad Horizon ♪♪♪♪♪♪♪♪

(Nota: 2012) **P.S. :** **¶ and Sound** are so familiar„ very similar to **Mussorgsky** ♪♪♪♪♪♪♪♪

*Une **Nuit sur le** Mont **Chauve*** ... ... A **Night** on the Bald **M**ountain ♪♪♪♪♪♪♪♪

7. Lahore: Punjab **A Study in Sounds** **Heard NOT Seen** (15 years – 1956 Mar.)

... ttps://www.pexels.com/search/balochistan%20Pakistan/ ... pexels-photo-3110502.jpeg ... pexels-photo-3726313.jpeg ...

... pexels-photo-210876.jpeg ... pexels-photo-1114690.jpeg ... pexels-photo-672636.jpeg ...

- X Axis = Time (seconds)
- Y Axis = Pressure

(Notice the zero point and the measure of amplitude.)

Sound and music are parts of our everyday sensory experience. Humans have **Eyes** for the detection of light and colour, as **Ears** for detection of sound, which is the **Physics of Waves**: created by vibrating objects, propagated through a medium from one location to another.

Waves are disturbances that travel through a **Medium**, transforming **Energy** from ***a Location to different Location***. A **Medium**'s simply a **Material**, through which **Disturbances** Move; it can be thought of as, **Series of Interacting Particles**. A **Slinky Wave**, is to be illustrated! **Nature of a Wave**. A disturbance is typically created, when within the **Slinky**, by back and forth movements, of the **First Coil of Slinky**. The first coil becoming disturbed begins to **Push or Pull the Second Coil**. This push or pull on the second coil**, Starts Displacing**, the second coil from its **Basic Equilibrium Position**. The second coil self-displacing, begins **Pushing or Pulling**, the **Third Coil ...** & so on.

A sound wave is similar in nature to a slinky wave. **1**. A medium carrying a disturbance from one location to another; air, water or steel; a series of interconnected and interacting particles. **2**. An original source. **3**. Particle-to-Particle Interaction. Thus it's a mechanical wave.

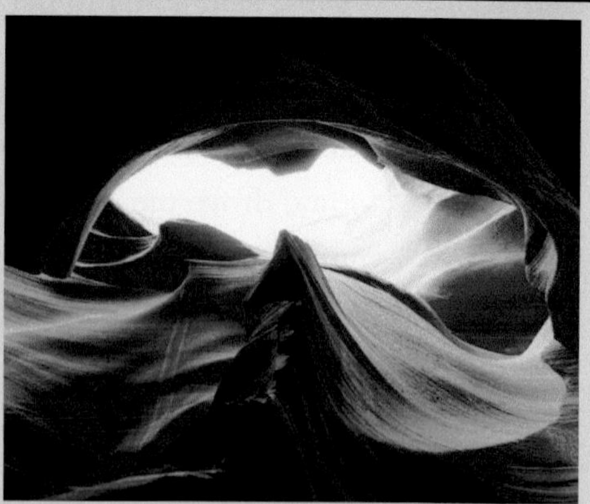

... pexels-photo-327509.jpeg ... pexels-photo-1719233.jpeg ... pexels-photo-342002.jpeg ...

7. Lahore: Punjab **A Study in Sounds** **Heard NOT Seen** (15 years – 1956 Mar.)

7. Lahore : Punjab **A Study in Sounds** Heard NOT Seen (15 years – 1956 Mar.)

He heard his name whispered softly behind.

" Is that you? " **" Un hum "**

" Why did you leave the hall so abruptly! They wanted you to play some Music.
Many are even shouting for you now. "

" Haven't you *Hurt* me enough to follow me even out here! "

" I didn't *Hurt* you. Only you didn't talk to me that day and … "

The sentence remained unfinished as a soft slithering tread a little way off, passed in a straight line towards the left,, crunching a few Stones, which from the sound seemed to lie indistinctly strewn about in a grassy patch. A hurried conversation about changing guard was soon Lost. But they both remained Silent,, listening to the song of the crickets which resembled the humming tune of a doleful tambura.

" Why are you sitting out here all alone ? "

" Their half–tone Life and half-heart Laughter disgusted me. Even now I can't get its ring out of my ears. " What he had actually wanted to reply was, " Because your Beauty was evoking unsaid *Jealousies*", but I just couldn't, just couldn't … stay!

Shyness is ineffable, hiding its indecisions quietly to bear them.

After a while he said, " Do sit down. "

" I'll spoil my clothes. " **" So what! "**

He held out his hand but didn't press hers too hard. *Defiant moods, effort to be brutal towards the affections, but the plans of shyness lie off dormant.* From Time to Time, variously pitched sounds continued unobtrusively for short intervals from obscure sources all over while she sat down where she felt the small stretch of coarse **sand** was smoothed,, and her bare feet tingled pleasantly at the rude buss of the plashing Water. The Words 'coarse and **grey**', 'coarse and **grey**' echoed in her **Mind** again 'n again 'n again, but she didn't know why? Why. **It was just another of those never explained thoughts, which slumber in the Human Brain.**

" I didn't mean to *Hurt* you. Only that day you had come in looking raggéd and wouldn't talk to me … so **Naturally** I didn't either. " **" I was feeling miserable. "** **" Why? "**

" Because: sometimes one does 'n there's no explaining to it. Hasn't one any right to act **miserable** … when one feels, that the heart by force has been wrenched out from you. **Nothing** might happen,, but trifles unimportant build up 'n one feels **lonely** all suddenly. **Sometimes** one has an incomparable feeling of having Lost **Something Somewhere**. *As **Happiness** 'n Sadness sleep entwined in **Human** beings, so does **loneliness*** … thus to gaze upon these patterns encircling us … to disintegrate 'n mingle into the **Universe** in all its grandeur,, so's to find out as such our **True** vocation. Friendship is understanding and lies deeper than **W**ords„ thus thought I, you would understand and forgive me. But the next day you snubbed me; so I went home and I Cried. "

It was good he had so done„ because imprisoned **E**motions wither and leave one without **Human** companionship! He had flung himself **f**ace down on his bed and pressed a pillow to his **c**hest„ the pressure thus exerted seemed rather to hold his heart which was ready to burst. Realization of unfulfilled **Love** wrecks one's **World** and one's heart„ and in this 'Waste **desolated land**', pulsate the ***Broken*** pictures of the past, of slight **Hop**es of recovering **So**mething dear **L**ost become all the more ***Painful***, because more than **half the World rests on Hop**es **which are never realized**. *Opportunity dangles before a shy person„ only to be clad well in Doubts at his own* **Happiness**. He always had a definite feeling that she liked him„ but **F**eelings easily are distraught.

" I'm sorry. "

She sounded much disturbed; thus the unconscious dabbling of her **l**egs flowing into intersecting curves, slowed the splatter„ may-be due to the unexpected plunk he had created, by throwing a Pebble into the Water purling through the Reeds. In the cool **breeze** these Reeds crackled, as the spray raised smelt fresh„ blown **Lightly** onto their **W**arm **f**aces. At all angles in the air, spread creaks 'n pitters„ and the resonance of these creaking pitters 'n patters, made itself felt with a gentle touch on the **e**ar, while further the amorous croaks of frogs, extended longingly longly into **S**ilence.

" NO. **Be not sorry.** I'm to blame too. " " **NO**. But please come in now. "

" Un-hum. Not yet. Tell me how did you know I'd he here ? "

" Do you remember how **So**metimes we used to sit here for long ***H****ours* and heard many **animals L**iving their **lonely** lives? And you used to assure me, that the crawling I was afraid of was **N**othing more than a mole or a rabbit at the worst„ and that the dull splotches were just the spurning trout rising from the depths„ trying to catch a trout-bug or a fly, which at best are a nuisance anyway. And there we used to **L**augh aloud. And once when we were caught out in a sudden shower, our damp clothes clung to our **s**kin as we ran for shelter„ and you saved me many a **T**imes, when I stumbled o'er the steps crumbling directly behind us. **How sweet flowers smell aft a slight** mis**F**ortune. And already, ***R****eality seems like slipping off, into the obscure patches of* ***M****emory.* "

Far to the **E**ast arose the confused voices of men, who as they were sailing away with the current, veered around to avoid some snag„ thus forming a smallish triangle of sound. The boat Lantern was not visible, may be it was as yet unlit so one could see not anything„ but still the strains of a plaintive d♪♫y (ditty) were wafted towards them in an aroma of **R**omance and **S**adness. The moon closed its **e**yes, 'n ***F****ire-****F****lies* went to sleep.

They listened intently and then he mumbled, "Beautiful **F**eelings **remain too cruel to afford Pleasure in any realm other than** Art. You play on an instrument and feel Beautiful ♪¶us♪c; but do you know what rent the heart of the strings that they weep so.

One's Misery is another's Pleasure:

like the flowers which burn their hearts out to incense the World. "

" If the heart be *Broke*, what matters what else be mended or *Broke*. "

She understood: though she heard only a few **W**ords.

Their **E**motions seemed to echo the ruffled **Peace 'n Harmony** in the susurrus of the sighing **ripples** overlapping the faint rumple of the **leaves**. No warble ***Broke*** the uneven quietness lying in the hues of shining **Star-LIGHTS**. From the **bowels** of the apparently calm sphere the almost unperceived Tremors of an **Earth**quake gently chased one another in quick succession„ and equalized in sympathy with the disproportionate jolt of **E**motional stress, which inverts the displaced senses from clear perception. He had a feeling of a light caress on his **h**and. He moved close to her and both sensed in **Reflections**, **T**ears in each other's **e**yes.

The soul can never be spoken, but by the Shadow **windows of the e**yes.

They saw **No**thing but felt everything. ***Love** is most evident when **f**aced with strife.* Then he fumbled with her **wr**ist„ and with her **n**ail sketched on his opened **p**alm '**three simple Words**': only three simple **W**ords. The hurried business–like buzz of a mosquito probably, circled around and went unnoticed in **S**ilence„ and so appearing diagonally from the **S**outh-**W**est was the overhead flapping of a tired noctule, bound to some unknown **D**estiny. A nyctalopic moth bumped against them, as if asking them to move over; but **thought** better of it and left. Then, some way-less insect crept up his **a**rm; to be was flicked off with a snip of the **f**ingers. From the sanctuary of some ruined wall a self-satisfied mew after a chase defied an increasing chorus of eager barks, till a supressed grumble was audible near the guard-house„ and a shoe thumped against a few loose **R**ocks which clattered thinly down. Then for a moment, *all became sound 'n **S**ilence simultaneously existing and evanescent, like **L**ife's disintegrated **Peace** 'n **Harmony**.* On the other side hung faintly in the **N**orthward air a serried series of confined roars like zoo-roars, but it vanished **completely**. The **Earth** exhaled an after-rain fragrance and from the cradle of some unseen weeds and foliage, the incessant varied noises of the hidden crickets mingled with a few sparsely spread-out pitters swelled and faded inconstantly, in a lazy **Rhythm**. Along with all this rose from the right a streaky **D**isturbance running parallel to the **Shore**, to delve under-**G**round. About the same instant an untimely crowing lengthened long; long along **Somewhere in the** far-**G**round **of undistinguished sounds**.

" Come on let's go back. They must be leaving.

I don't hear anymore the **R**ocking and crashing of Music and doors are being slammed. "

" O must we. They said there was to be an eclipse shortly,

but I wonder why the moon hasn't come up yet. "

" **Hang the moon**. " His tone was all **S**miles ... and he continued ...

" There goes the clock in our square. Before we can start for home we'll have to

climb all those stairs. Now if you ever stumble you'll always have me to lean on. "

Cross the **Waves** the town **silhouette** lay misty 'n deeply asleep! Wake up later 'twill, 'n go 'bout 'tis business. The private habitations were half-hid in the undulations of the indistinct boscage soaked in Mystery.

Only occasionally did the drowsy honks of an isolated horn tried to compete with the long hoots of a fine thin rail-whistle accompanying an efferent rumble which around the **W**estern bend, puffingly passed over the **Water** and continued on in it's snaky rectilinear motion„ till a while after it slowed and at its **N**ortherly destination screeched to a stop as the clanks and thuds of a workshop, also wove irregularly into a strange pattern of the **devil's** tattoo beat slowly on the bass drums. The faint Stream of the few motorcars kept on vibrating to and fro into all directions. The last song from a drive-in theatre was not inaudible„ as was dissolved into the notes of a factory siren coming from half-way to the right and far back. It started from thick and dipped to a **Lighter** and **Lighter** higher key subsiding soon to the original heavy note and thus inverted unreasonably gave an absurd sonic effect of a large top-side-down sound cone. And on account of the distance, all the strident noises appeared as proceeding from miniature toys. Presently, mechanical staccatos of a motorbike came closer and closer o'er the **Water**, 'n then arced outwards: the throb of its **S**ilencer-less engine seemed to be in unison with the inner beating in his heart. *Unexpected* ***Happiness*** *derails the train of* **Mind** *into strange tunnels.* Instantly the ticking of his **w**rist-watch re**Minded** him„ **that every precious thing must** Die**, because 'twas born.**

He got up and said to her, " I feel like **L**oving you all the years in **Infinty** and a *few moments more„* then to be with you to the end of **Eternity** and *a little beyond.* And if you ever become **A**ngry, I'd raise the last breath in my **b**ody to do you service and **change thy** Frown **to a** Smile-let. But then I'd be giving back to you **Nothing** more than what is already thine„ for I inspire of thy breath of purest **thoughts** and so take my entire **b**eing from thee. You have heard of the **flower** which **L**ives in the countenance of the Sun and of the Stars, which always revolve closely around one another„ but you have never heard of one who feels **W**retched, because **these comparisons seem finite** and somewhat separate. When we are **alone** I think of the moon and dream of thee„ and in this dream we are like **P**articles of the mizzling moon-smut dissolved in the spumy crest of a Dangerous billow carried along endlessly into the slum-full folds of liquid depths„ till I awake suddenly up, to find my so fine a moon-beam **C**rystallised become like the **oyster**'s **Treasure**„ **the Pearl of existence**. The **lonely oyster L**ives only for its **Pearl**„ thus I'd live sucking on a moon-drop, *dreading that someday* ***Somebody*** *may come to take you away from me.* To be always with you, I want to crush you to myself to almost become a part of me ...

... **for: there's ever an element of cruelty in Love„ 'n of** *Pain* **in Pleasure**.

O, but because what's thine's mine 'n mine thine„ I'd ask you not to hold your **h**and too tightly 'n make me wince. **O,** when you grow old, I'd give everything in the **World** for us to be young again. **O,** you are an exceedingly sweet child: my only **R**egret is that I knew you not in all that delightful delicious period. **O,** living in the liquid of your **e**yes„ that when you close them, the lingering *Tear*-lets scatter the fragments of my **Soul** to the four **W**inds„ and the fore **Earth** underneath. **O,** to be young once more at least in our **thoughts**. **O,** but when I again become agéd and apart myself have none left to give„ and so *together we'd rest leaving behind us a* ***M****emory, few* ***primroses*** *new 'n fresh„* as the changing seasons so constant, but never the same **bud** again. **O,** then in the murmur of the **W**inds, I'd re**Mind** you ...

O, how forlornly we sighed for each other, in other people's presence. "

" **Mm** ... You do speak such beautiful **thoughts**.

Only let a man win in Love, to see thus that all bounds become boundless.

I've never listened to so sweet words before. "

" Do you know Why? Because I've never known anyone like you before: to utter such **thoughts** to. I wish I had been a great **W**riter,, for **N**o-o**ne** else can express what unbounded **W**ords 'n **Worlds** of **thoughts** 'n **E**motions I feel, when I sink into these soft sweety **e**yes of yours,, a whole **Universe** confined to so little a **f**rame, unable to hold it.

Would that mine essence of experience had scented pages of fragrant Poetry. "

Nearby, an unidentified froggy, eavesdropping, overhearing this, glopped "**bouche bée**"; and was gone. A discontinued splash was all that was left, to remember him by. Hugging the **E**ast-most Horizon, hung a parabolic drone sound, coming to the end of its search for an aerodrome,, and it drowned all 'n even that. They moved away. Then as he st**oo**ped towards her, he was rebuked; as if 'twas to conquer?

" Stop it. " " **No**. Never. "

And finally when he kissed her she retorted teasingly, " You haven't shaved. "

" I'm a **Beast** ", he admitted happily ... and continued ...

" And I've always thought you to be the **Bestest Beautiful Beauty Babe** in the whole **World**. "

" I'm not. " She was **b**ubbling with **L**ife. " **One may never, need be pretty, to be in L**ove. "

" At least for me you are. That is, if you just could manage to l**oo**k a little or more or any less cross or cross-**e**yed **and** shifted your **n**ose a bit more **and** to the right **and** Lost a few extra pounds off your under-**c**hin **and** but do it s**oo**n **and** before it's t**oo** late **and** and **and** and ..."

" Nonsense. "

" Admitted. Yes. But a very **L**oving special kind of nonsense **and** ..."

" **O, shut up** ..." " **Okay, okay. But don't expect me to keep quiet and** ..."

And sidled close to her while the many sounds kept on being repeated variably,, like the auricular designs of ⁋¶us♪c,, and the crickets continued as ever in the long drawn manner of the enveloping four–stringed chords **and** accords of a sonorous pair of Tanpuras.

P.S. 2012 : As a Child, I **Loved** to roam around **Nights**,, by br**oo**k or Stream or street or beam ...

And I used to Hear a Lot of Sounds,, Hundreds of Sounds 'n Sounds ...

Sounds Remembered, Sounds Memorised 'n Sounds Recorded Innely ...

... **And Sounds became my e**ars **and my e**yes ...

... **So a Sound became also a Thought Intern** ...

Thinking,, if one day I Lost Sight ... I could **See in the Night** ...

... **See All Without LIGHT** ...

... 'Twas so I wrote a **Love** Story,, **Without** Any **Colour** or Any **N**o**thing** Bright,, never a Scene ...

... **Only Slightly** Seen the un-Seen of **Everywhere**,, Where I had **Never, Never *Ever* Never Been** ...

8. Karachi : Sindh **T'wink'ling Lights** (15 years – 1956 Aug.)

https://www.pexels.com/search/balochistan%20Pakistan/ ... pexels-photo-556665.jpeg ... pexels-photo-397278.jpeg ...

... https://www.pexels.com/search/Poetry/ https://www.pexels.com/photo/art-artistic-blank-page-book-371954/ ...3376178.jpeg

... https://www.pexels.com/photo/silhouette-photo-of-a-man-walking-on-seashore-during-sunset-3761178/ ... Sunset

Karachi, a small fisherman village of **Baloch** & **Makran** tribes, originally settlements being near **Indus River Delta**, named "**Kolachi**". The Community inhabited near the Port. British Raj recognized the importance of the city, as an important **Trade Post**. They thus, captured "**Kolachi**" and the Sindh Province in February **1843**, under command of Sir Charles Napier: the city being annexed, as district of British Indian Empire! **1st. direct Telegraph** Connection Message, in 1864, sent 'tween Karachi & **London**. **Pakistan**'s founder, Muhammad Ali Jinnah, born in **Kolachi** in 1876, Ismaili Khojas! Once asked Cleverly, **Which Sect**? Replied Cleverly; Sect: **Muhammad** (saw).

Karachi was chosen as the Capital of **Pakistan** in 1947. During this period, the city offered shelter to a huge influx of migrants and refugees that came from the Indian province. In 1960, the capital of **Pakistan** was moved later to Islamabad. Karachi never lost economic centre-ship of its founded **Pakistan**. cf. www.karachi.com/v/history/

England ... **London** ... **https://www.pexels.com/photo/old-ornamental-big-ben-facade-in-london-3954505/**

Faiz ... Karachi ... City of Lights

Roshniyon ka Sheher

I have the honour to have had

4 of the Greatest Teachers ...

Feroz **Nizami** [Classic Music]

Faiz Ahmed **Faiz** [Lenin Prize 1962]

Imtiaz Ali **Taj** [Best Urdu Dramatist]

Ahmed Mirza **Jamil** [Urdu Nastaliq]

https://www.pexels.com/search/Poetry/ ... https://www.pexels.com/photo/art-artistic-blank-page-book-371954/

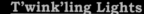

8. Karachi : Sindh **T'wink'ling Lights** (15 years – 1956 Aug.)

8. Karachi : Sindh **T'wink'ling Lights** (**15 years** – 1956 Aug.)

(Somehow I 'felt' that I may 'loose' my home-town 'forever' ... True Later)

Away down below the Horizon, swallowed up in tumultuous **Seas**,
Does my home-town lie„ as sail I, O away.
The gulls above fly, flying to their nests; to with their mates lie happy:
But my **Love**, I leave her so far behind.

The swallows flying homewards towards the cold **N**orth now„ tarry
in craggy **C**aves and **R**ocky **C**averns their short rest, make merry;
but for me even milder days press so heavy so **lone** „
for afar from one's home, the softest pillow feels the hardest Stone!

The fish, carol they in the deep; and **So**metimes from the **Ocean's** floor peep„
tender **a**rms entwined, in an-other's sleep:
but O my be**L**ovéd, I saw her then weep
when my boat out of the harbour i' th' gulf of **t'wink'ling LIGHTS**, did creep!
O! that I could reach her a**S**tray in my f**lights**„
of day's dreams: of **Night** dreams„ of fancies, of **Sights**.
Thus sailed I out away, on the breast of a heaving boundless **Sea**,
lying, in ¶ystery.

Which a moment seemed to stand still a-listening: Listening 'n ... **Thinking**„ **Thinking** 'n Pausing
in Confusion, Confused at the many, so many Riddles **L**ife Sows to Be-riddle **Human** Beings„
in their **Prime**: their **Youth**: their **Age**!

Silent, I looked on **f**rothy **f**lu**ff**y **f**urrowy **F**oams **f**ading **f**ar a**f**ar a**f**ay;
while around me lay, the company gay:
Winds playing on the mighty chest
which hoard, so countless a secret
of, thousands forgotten century, ne'er met.
And it moved restful 'n restless 'n forlorn,
by ***P****assions* not of **mortal** senses torn:
for what does man know which ***E****motions unknown„*
shake with ***S****ilent* ***T****ears, the seething bosom of the elements, so shorn.*

A couple nearby **L**aughed: and I **C**ry!
In one same spot lies gloom 'n joy
While only those enduring differ!
For ***bliss*** *for one's, a* ***blight*** *on another.*

Thus all is alike, be it good or ill;
Though a sullen mood brings the best to **nil**:
The will is all 'n all's man's will!

The ship kept sailing, its horn kept wailing;
The children ran playing, the youth kept braying;
The brides stopped dancing; the grooms went a-drinking;
The old began praying: 'n thus the **S**orrowful left a-brooding.
The moistened air was chiller, the **dark** blank **Sea** looked colder„
The second-mate came hither„ to slowly tap 'n tap me on the **s**houlder;
'Thee I pray, the sulken **Night** has fallen very **S**harp 'n long,
'They, of now, have sounded the last dinner gong!'

* * * * * *

The watch slowly was struck at one
The next day was begun;
The **Stars** dimmed,
The **Waves** brimmed„
Then **rippled** as dull chimes.
There under these **Skies**,
Thus the sad **lone Soul** flies„
To the home-town's dear climes!

O'er **H**ill 'n **Dale** the **Spirit S**torms
And borne along is all o'er the **F**oams„
Must return but to prisonous body's bin
For in Life **all one does, is a lot of Sin.**

I looked down 'n mirrored in the **rippling** dimpled **Waters** of the **Ocean** hush
Winked the **S**tars as the spritely ***Fire-Flies*** hiding in the **leaves** of the **rose**-bush:
The tiny impish **S**tars embedded in the milky **Sky**„
Jewelled loosely on **darkish** crest of scattered-**W**aves by
Clustering like gems around the shy rising moon stand-by
As **P**earls a-strewn in the **l**ocks of a **L**ovely **Fæy**„
Matched soft moon-**LIGHT** on **Watery** twirls that shower pale,
The way **Glimmering Diamonds emBellish** the **Beauty** of a **Belle**!

A **Belle** who stays **lone**, pines afar from me
Gazing in a haunting **Charm** of chanting murmuring **Sea**!
I seek to the **E**ast, the **P**ath from where I came
Ô hush! On the far off edge, the **Watery** frame
Ô see! Lo behold a distant blinking ***Flame*** ...

... Merging out of the **Sea**; merging thus from and into the **Sea** afore
The distant **lonely** flash **alone**; does spout a swarm of more
Glistering on the **ripples** which gulp these *Sparks* on *Fire*
Floating in **black** depths„ a swaying replica of heights
Glittering Flickering Shivering images of **LIGHTS**
Rising from the **Sea**; rising above the **Sea**
The **LIGHTS** 'n eidolæ coalesce:
Blinking twinking, blinking twinkling
Lumined forms
as **glow**-Worms„
im**Pearling** the **Ocean**
and studding **Water**'s motion„
quivering **Rays Shivering** shinier **Waves**
than planktons in the **darks** which invade
the weedy-**grey**, **Night**-haunts of any mermaid.
The ship-deck throbbing but still
The twin-moons ascending up until,
And sleepy, the **Stars** are drowsing„
The multitudes of *Fires* ever arising
Dancing **Glimmering** gay-fully jingling
Nearer clearer the **Myriads** winking
Chiming tinking chiming tinkling:
A wonder wondrous: a wondrous wonder!

The veils do ope and reveal my city left without **Hope**
of seeing, again in years to cope.
One by one my companions come to greet me 'n bid me farewell„ 'n I nod to them all 'n sacred.
But I search a small door of a house in a dell, where **L**ives my be**L**ovéd:
She passed by; and raised her fair **h**and to **pinky L**ips„ and blew a dream kiss!

O! that I could melt into my Love
That the past and the future may blend ... And that the Time**, then be ended!**

The populace of **Flickering Lamps**, whose interplay shone for a few minutes from a passing craft, drown into the swirly deeps of the **Shady Marine**. The visages grow **hazy** 'n waver 'n dissolve ℙ¶ysterꝭously in the **oneiric** Dimness **of a Nowhere where reside all that we once had**, but have no more! O, a blessing 'twill be, if **Sometimes** we ceased to **Think**„ and in the *Hours* of **loneliness** be not disturbed by any airy countenances most adored, repeating the same pounding **Emotional** **W**ords, which echo persistently from the folds of **M**emory, as distorted **husky whispers** engulfing a **Night**-mare: *to make a **Mind** a **Hell** of its own **Creation**„*

'n living with oneself the worst Hell there is.

Thus they with best meaning, come to console us in intangible dreams„ a dream or child of one's vaporous **Mind**, a Phantom of one's **D**esire: **Nothing** more than an **A**nguish of one's torn heart!

And then beyond the dim **S**hadows of the floats, these longings glide 'n sway away„
into the oblivion of **Night**
far from that which is bright„
leaving no traces
of our **Loved Lost f**aces:
of the absent, the **M**emory sweet, is tinged with ***Pain***„
of Happiness unshared, a lonely burden so hung twain!

The **glows** do vanish and the days do banish the **nocturnal** spell„
Which brings to the **Mind**, the Vision of the **Sights** now endeared so well.
O, swifting away so far away ... **one by one by one**„ as the *Hours* do pass,
From the Shaded glen where cuckoo-calls are coy„ where spreads silky-grass,
Beyond brimming brooks be-running by briskly, besides but bubbling blithely„
Down the **H**ills which lie in **ripplets**„ and the peaks o'er which triplets glisten snowy;
Where bees do hum 'n the **flowers** give forth so fragrant **Colours** sweetly:
Hues of **silver** play in the **blue Sky** and the **S**tars do twinkle brighter„
A-**Shimmering** in **Lustrous** dew-drops„ scattered in a **leafy** cloister.

There we roamed beneath **clouds** floating in cool **Winds„ best Love philtre**.
Coloured mists flow in and hide it„ in the thinly **P**ainted hazy wispy curtains„
From the air than arose ⁋¶elod♪ous smooth tones„ as all faded in **Magic**-strains.
In the bay of soft **Flickers**: nests this vernal **I**sle of twinking twinkling lowly **LIGHTS**„

My home-town!

On the airy wings of the dove, my heart does fly,
To the waiting **a**rms of my restless be**L**ovéd„ gently awaiting by.

It has been years since I thus embarked on the **lonesome** voyage: comfortless; comfortless except for un-soothing **M**emories of the enkindled past. Around me, soft **eddies ripple** ⁋¶us♪c on **R**ocks embedded in these calms, resplendent of so soothing restful **sands** ...

*"You are young and of **Love** you are full„ 'n yearn to gift it all: till you are left pure **null!**"*
How swift does **T**ime fleet, leaving us past moments as blanks to be filled in by Fancy!

Maybe 'twas True Love or 'twas not„ but left her I did„ 'n only I feel, what I felt.

My **World** has ***Broke***„ so lots of **T**imes„ and at such **T**imes, I go and drown myself ... in the

Twinkling **R**efl**e**ctions of **N**ights 'n **B**rights ... 'n in all these **Twinking LIGHTS** ...

9. Lahore: Punjab Images : **A Rhythm of a Mind** (15 years – 1956 Dec.)

… https://pixabay.com/images/search/brain%20waves/ … quantum-physics-4550602__340.jpg …
… https://pixabay.com/vectors/brain-mental-health-think-5398414/ …

Frequency Band	Frequency	Brain States
Gamma (γ)	>**35 Hz**	Concentration: Acute
Beta (β)	12–**35 Hz**	Anxiety Domain: Active
Alpha (α)	08–**12 Hz**	Very Relaxed: Passive
Theta (θ)	04–**08 Hz**	Deep Relaxed: Inward
Delta (δ)	0.5–**4 Hz**	Sleep: *Subconscious*

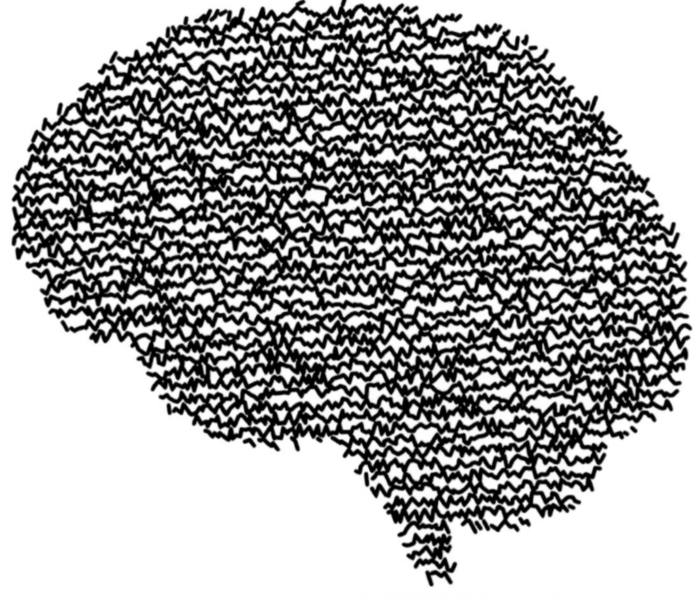

Stop struggling and you will float in the Universe.

If there is light in the soul, there will be beauty in the person.

If we don't make time for our lives, our lives won't make time for us.

Who is talking inside you? Spirit says: "Find peace and everything will fall into place."

… The biggest communication problem is … We do not Listen to Understand … We Listen to Reply …

The '7 Wonders of the World' …**1**. to **See** **2**. to **Hear** **3**. to **Touch** **4**. to **Taste** **5**. to **Feel** **6**. to **Laugh** and **7**. to **Love** …

"Nature soon takes over if
the gardener is absent."
PENELOPE HOBHOUSE

… https://pixabay.com/images/search/lightning/ … pexels-photo-1118873.jpeg …
… https://www.pexels.com/photo/quote-on-signboard-on-shabby-wall-near-bright-green-leaves-4371730/ … Penelop Hobhouse …

9. Lahore : Punjab — Images: **A Rhythm of a Mind** (**15 years** – 1956 Dec.)

Once upon a Time, far beyond where so dappled
Clouds do hide the Mountain tops, a land of *Fæys*
Did exist. In this, the Never-Neverland of Fancy
And imagination, all the year round where
Forever, in a State of Continuous Now„
SpringTime did **L**ive mellow 'n the Autumn never
Came„ except to **Paint** the Trees in **pretty Colours**
Of the **Iris** in the Down of Heron's Feathers
Where lavender and **rose**-like aura tint'd the midday
Air; and no Birds stopped their singing, till the children
Went to bed: where furry pets frolicked around„ in tepid
Sunshine, in **Glades Sprouting** with so many **flowers**
Like the **Iridesence** in the **Edges** of any **Prism**; and
Where **Stars** be-studded by a **Sapphire** moon changed
As many hues as small **RAINBOWs** decking the **Sky**
In the coolness of the Wintery evening : in this
Little Land, of sweet **Night**'s always fragrant
With **Love** ... Lived **alone** a **pretty** little child with
Star-like **e**yes„ 'n **c**heeks, that radiated health.
One can never always keep **L**iving on in imagination
And must wistfully scale the depress of **R**eality,
He grew **lonely** and **lonelier** and left the fæery-land
To be born in this World„ *to seek so after **Happiness***.

* * * * * *

He was born anew in a picturesque Valley ... bound on three sides by high Mountains. It opened out, and from a rise in the middle was visible the great **Lake** with the contours of its farthest **Shore** mingling into the line of the Horizon. It was here that the **Sun** set and the wavy disc rose up from the emicant **Waters**„ to vanish into the flat of the igneous **Sky**line, **Lightening** the Dimness beyond: and just an instant before **dark**, the snowy peaks and the near **Edges** of the flecks of mottled white and **grey clouds** became a diffused **pink**„ to stand out distantly as papier–mâché symbols against the emollient **blue** of the cold **Sky**. Towards the **W**est where the ***B**roken* layers of Liard **clouds** were thicker than usual, many **Colours** from the **Paint**-box of **Nature** were spilt across the **Sky**„ while nearer the Water lilac and yellow tints were limned upon the sides with **the symmetry of chance combinations**. And just above the fuzzy Horizon, the fleecy velum of molten **gilt** was slashed across so, that the reflection of the refulgent **Sun** was streaked right across the **Lake** as an orange blur disturbed by the ripples of its red reddish **R**ays, striated all the **Sha**d**es** of verdant in the sprog-high growth 'n more. And all this ambient **Beauty** of the **Myriads** of melting **Colours** in the changing air„ was photographed and printed onto the uneven surface of the **Lake**„ the margins of which were bordered by the tall lengthy **S**ilhouettes of **bistre**-tanned **Trees** under the **S**hadows of the **S**crubs 'n the Clouds.

It was on such an evening that he walked upon the green on his way to the fair-**G**rounds. And so he passed the ancient **R**uins which were discovered some hundreds of years back near the old town: then he paused in his stride. He was thinking that *since the beginning of motion, immeasurable* **Oceans** *of Time have flowed on„ to* ***no-one*** *knows where*, leaving behind **No**thing but decay: like Liana upon **R**ocks„ **out of** Death **springs forth L**ife, to be again swallowed up into annihilation„ *thus posing the problem of the* ***past*** *and the* ***present*** *and the* ***future*** *and why everything happens as it does.* Thru **present** beholding **past**, he found himself sitting on a **Lagan**„ where lay before his **e**yes mounds and heaps of breccia, the Lichened **R**elics of a once magnificent structure„ and in his **Soul** all the grandeur of the **past** concentrated into one flighting moment; ***and he saw*** *Visions* ***of* majestic emperors courting defeat in the splendour of its fall**: and he had Doubts that they had actually gone by and a**L**ive no more„ ***for R****emembrance* ***is a token of immortalilty.*** Then his **Mind** turned to commoner and commoner **f**aces; and he remembered his Dead teacher who had learned him his trade„ 'twas an untutored but a wise man: *there are greater philosophers 'mongst peasants than amongst scholars;* for he was born to that **Natural** philosophy, which if delineated from the cause and purpose of its originator ... unrecorded will Die out with him. Like the laws of **Nature** everlasting and unobtrusive, he always used to be near and always around, and then he wasn't„ he went so far away that he ceased to exist! Without any warning or without any explanation„ the premature expiration of all his interests, leaving behind the chasm **No**thing but just a few images engaged in everyday toils„ with no answer to the question, " *Where does everything go?* " **a riddle as insoluble as God**.

And he lamented why at an in**experienced** age he had not taken the advice of the older man, when out of excessive exuberance he had flirted with a girl towards whom he hadn't ever been seriously inclined. He wouldn't have **Minded** her being not so good-looking, as due to her devotion he considered himself already pledged to her„ but she was uninteresting as well and **completely** extraneous to his **T**emperament. And he felt himself to be a misfit and left her. Then he hated himself for years, to withdraw into a **SHELL** of self-torture„ where the **W**ords of his tutor constantly hammered away at his conscience:

" Never do ***Hurt*** anyone, specially a not so **pretty** a woman„

for the *Coal* **may consume to** Dust **and never be changed to** Dia**m**o**n**ds. "

Considering himself as instrument in the **D**estruction of a fellow being's **Hop**es, he determined to punish himself as severely as he had ***Hurt*** her. Adolescents tend to be infatuated towards someone particular: now he even forwent his unuttered infatuation towards another„ and though each such friendship seldom bears Fruit in maturity, yet they are very ***Painful*** to relinquish in the freshet of strange **E**motions. Search after ***Happiness*** leads through **T**horny **P**aths„ because ***fickleness confuses Happiness with gratification.*** Ironically, an early **M**emory of child-hood came to him: "***Why am I born***?" "Not to suffer like others!" was his answer to this simple puzzle.

When he had considerably overcome his mental conflict of "encraty" (incrustation)„ he had met another one, who seemed not to care sufficiently for him, but still lead him on. A heart which *Breaks* others was itself *Broken* once, like the **D**estructive pieces of that Rock hardened under the plunge of the same **Waterfall** which destroyed it. She had been jilted Once upon a Time„ and had made it a point to jilt all else that she could. She found him cold, but left him weak: only recently had she bade him a last good-bye, thwarting his tentative attempts to confide in **Somebody** and feel a part of **Something**. Had his tutor been a**L**ive, he would have analysed this situation as: *"Woman has a protective instinct to always have her womb full and become possessed of a child.* ***Man is born of this mother„ the one loses its inmate, the other it's shelter****„ and like the affinity of an atom for a similar valency, all his **L**ife is a search for a womb in the image of his mother to go back into and hide in from the cares of the **World**, to be knurled as much as he needs:* ***and from these Stray encounters, arise the constancy and inconstancy of Life."*** **L**ife now had crossed two steps: first of *'being introduced to **Love**'* ... second of being made to *'know what **Love** is not'* ... and he only needed an else one to come along and reveal to him the **Infinte** possibilities of the simple **World 'Love'**: third ... But he himself would be the first to deny such a case: he considered himself able to dis*Passionately* control the workings of his **E**motions. Potentialities hold strange surprises in store, for one is never perfectly aware of what one really wants.

Absorbed in his **thoughts**, he realised that he already was half-way down the slope, when through a *Tear* in the **clouds** he saw a bright **S**tar shining on the tension of the still **Waters**„ and his **lonesome** mood identified himself with its aloofness. *At the **D**awn of **Universe** the vesper **Star** **L**ost a companion and thus it stands **alone** like a constant **Lover**, to the ends of **Creations**„* thinking that the image at the bottom of the pellucid **Lake**, whose **Edges** droop with narcissus Florets **S**miling up from the **Water**, would rise once and be united to him forever: forever hoping„ realizing not that **in the darkness of** ***Pain*****, Glimmers of Hope enhance the gloom**„ because *Suffering only becomes endurable when no **Happiness** is held out.* And as strange **thoughts** are often clothed in adequate surroundings, slowly the tiers of the hachured landscape, a paysagist's masterpiece, were drenched in the oncoming **Night**: the Meadow-like grass spread like a velvet cushion along the fringe of the specular lagoon„ and the erogenous **S**crubs spearing the undulations of the receding **H**illocks and the Pines rising in the heights, were all dissolved in the impending **dark**, while contingent **Lightening** from invisible sources played on the gradually **black**ening **Sky**„ which a moment before had seemed intensely **blue**,

like a monotone film of oil on a diaphanous pool.

Then in the distance he saw a blaze of **LIGHTS**,

like the **Irides** in laminated interiors of **SHELLS** mingling into

the randy whites of mother-of-**Pearl**; then picked his way, to awaiting fair-**G**rounds.

He passed a ***Fire*** **burning red** 'n **glowing**, as a **L**amp in a **dark**-room. A fake **Magician** wearing a flowing strange robe stood by„ and from **T**ime to **T**ime besprent some powder into the ***Fire***, that with a ***Flare*** everything was hued a monotint of **brown**. And children de**lighted**. The noise that lay around him, seemed as all were sound pictures, where the repercussive hustle of the crowd would appear like the track on a **S**moked **P**aper

of a seismograph needle run **W**ild!

Somebody *Fired* a rocket and high-up it burst

into a mushro-om of individually glowing Particles, as tracks of LIGHT in overexposed pictures of *Fire*-Worms: then all a seven Colour lying in cuts of a mirror, kept growing duller as the glaze of Nacreous Shades in powdered glass. And when he lo-oked down, he gazed straight into the **e**yes of a maiden, shy like a frightened reindeer ... Losing all her companions in the turbulent crowd. Then suddenly the total of his amative aspirations objectified in her **f**igure„ that he could intuitively visualise her in all her mo-ods to read the Tempers of her Mind. And his being seemed to draw near hers„ that were she a lump of sugar he would be inclined to lap it up.

She was dainty and graceful like a færy skimming on the edge of the breeze, kissing nectar with tender Lips from skeiny petals. All the continuous forms of Beauty in the **Sky** to-ok their depth and Lustre from her **blue** **e**yes. The crowning tresses framed upon her flushed **f**ace were soft as the substance of the **black** **Night** gliding by with Stars in her Hair; and they fell about her delectable **n**eck with the gentlest possible care, as if they possessed her and would protect her from coming to any *Harm*. Into her guileless Smile flowed all the sweetness in Heaven; while she to-ok the simplicity of her blush from the movements of pink Butterflies flitting over the god-ripe for an innocent kiss. Her **e**arlobes were punctured like flaws in a gem„ but there rested ruby–studded Stars of schilling gold, brighter than her Pearl-ivory **t**eeth. Her **s**houlders were of the smo-othness of wax and butter„ and so her seemly **b**reasts, of cotton–soft curd of coconut, rounder than any maid's, must have made even God blink in unbelief. A modestly cut shirt emphasized her usually high Spirit's in each curve of her healthy **b**ody. *A jealous woman had said of her that she had feline Charms of being stroked behind the* ***e****ar:* but her Charms were more the Charms reeking with innocence of being vivaciously aLive, of being full of an animated gaiety as the Reflections upon a blank wall of skeins, of LIGHT in Water„ and of being totally unconscious of this all; of the Charms in the freshness of a Mountain **W**ind playing in the Conifers and in the permanent and constant rumble mumble of the Mountain–Water. *When God created woman, 'Tis stole a rib„ 'n then carved in secret, by* ***Night****:* **but this lady, was the work of a Sunny after-no-on, when the Rays of the Aster were moulded into a Beauteous form„** for in her shape was the open **W**armth of a bright day flowing in all its splendour! Such was she when he first saw her, with Tears **rolling** down into her **e**yes: the prettiest thing that ever was ... wholly unmade for Tears but appearing so much **Lovelier** as a lily ... on whose sad petals two quivering droplets of dew Reflect the RAINBOW in the **Sky** ...

A visible concentration of ***Nature*** *in all her innocence and in all her simple Beauty!*

For him this was a moment of rhapsodic **E**motions. Everything else seemed to blur out; and she alone remained Sharp in the focus of **R**eality, with the Lamp-glows Glistering in her moistened **e**yes„ selectively standing out in relief against a distorted back-Ground composed of blobs of dancing LIGHTS, like the film of spectra rings in a stretched soap bubble projected on a wide screen.

And gradually this blown-up back-Ground of Prismatic Taints in the corny rictuses of a cracked plate of glass, well so well Sharpened„ that the details of the Iridesence were markedly visible through her superimposed idol, slowly parted in two visive images; and in this state of diplopia he wondered why he never had any multi-Coloured dreams... **One's dreams are oft in the photographic scale of grey,**

for no Sharp Radiance is Refracted in the Camerated antas of the Mind.

And he remembered last **Night** when he kept on sailing on the turbid sluggish River of his dream; seen from the **Shore**, through the distorted perspective piercing into the **Sky**, of tall Reeds whose motionless **Reflections** seemed like Stalks going down into the Water, he saw a disproportionately small boat capsizing in the distance: they all clambered back but counted one as missing„ among his dripping friends he found himself to be absolutely dry and had a queer sensation of **being aLive but not Living, active but not present**; then **Somebody** had pointed out that **Somehow** a raven had come in from **Somewhere** and sat down with them„ and frivolously he **thought** that supposing he was that raven; *frivolousness often leads to seriousness„* and suddenly he confronted himself before the mirror in his closet Almira and the enlarged image with a conspicuous **dark** medley of 'tis spittled graininess, was that of a huger than huge crow. So woke he immediately up, aware of **experiencing** a stark Fear„ where he knew there was **Nothing** to be afraid of, for it was all a dream! And he felt like the child who sat by the **darkness** of the smouldering ***Hearth*** and described **pretty** circles in the air with a **glowing** straw„ while his grandmother told him not to play with ***Fire*** or he would have bad dreams. **What a Magic there is in children's stories**: ***and their Truth is forever present in the Human unconscious***. But now he also was afraid, afraid that the dream might ***Break***!

Laughter ***Broke*** in upon his reverie„ and he saw her among the whole bevy of her friends who had found her. *So oft it chances that* mis**F**ortunes *deemed the greatest are the slightest.* And he felt that she was the one thing that he had always been in search of„ the only thing that could **Complete** the meaning of **L**ife: and it had been like the meeting of the raven and the dove ... for all of them had lo-oked at him and **Laughed**! ***Sensitive people always hold themselves to be the cause of any jest or sport***. Then he saw their group move away and melt into the crowd. He had **Lost** what had not even been gained: and he felt hated and **abandoned**: and he **thought** that the only possible answer any impartial passer-by would give to his **Cry**, "Why am I despised", would be, "Because you have **Loved**!" He belonged to those few ***Passionate*** **Natures**, who dream up an **Idea** out of their bitter **experiences** and are ready to sacrifice the sum of **L**ife for that **Ideal**. He had known her for so short a while only, but she had become an obsession. And she became obsession„ maybe because he knew her for such a short while. On his recapitulations then, *intruded a picture of an evening-***Star** ***dejected*** *in the glory of an early morning.*

It was now that he met a friend who seemed to have undergone a great strain and embarked on a long tale as how yester evening he had met a girl, who ended the rest of the **World** for him„ but he had **Lost** her in the crowd and so had he **Lost** his **World** from below his **f**eet: and he added tersely, "How oft we wish that our cruel mistress could see us in the depth of our mis**F**ortune; and then cut in rather nonchalantly with, "You know I've always wanted to write **Poetry**. Well one must never let go the train of **Hope**, for this may yet transform me into a **R**omantic; a poët, a dreamer: in fact, a **Nothing**."

They often remain merry, who oftener are unhappy.

And our protagonist's being seemed to go out fully for his friend.

We sympathize with people's **S***orrow when our own is exhumed:*

Wretched**-ness draws near, 'tis self-**Wretch**-ness**.

And as thus, then he continued in equal strain, "In my heart resides a doll-like miniature of hers„ only she is much less cruel and in my ***Hours*** of **loneliness** keeps me company with her ingenious sweet 'n gay 'n happy prattle: then she kisses me good-bye and cuddles off to sleep„ while I gaze on her long after and tenderly caress her with the sincerest of sincere **E**motions."

What we feel has ever been felt by others who have suffered even more so. And he had a vague misgiving that both were thinking of the same person. In desperate moments we Doubt our sincerest friends, *because the instinct of self-preservation goads us on to be selfish.* But to retain his sanity he drove this **thought** from his **Mind**„ recollecting the Ruins which some illustrious king had raised in **M**emory of his dear mistress; then involuntarily in a fumigating resignation, the lines of a famous poët escaped his caution: "**An Emperor leant 'pon the staff of his Wealth„ Deriding the Love that utter we poor men can't by Stealth**." And his friend just gave him a quizzical look and said not a chant. All of us are kids and becoming so unreasonable, can't be understood: neither do we like to be„

*for some of us, live in a private **World** beyond the **S**tars: and will there remain always.*

Soon he left his friend, to go and sit in idle rumination in his shop„ where he saw their group advancing and coming to his counter; she asked the price of a turquoise ...

Replying he said, that she could have it for free.

"How?"
"***Only, if you ask me*** for it!"
"And if I ask for this one over here„ would you to me give it free,
that too?" She started being impish.
"Yes!"
Then she kept on asking about another and another and various other ones ...
receiving as always 'n ever, the same answer.
"And if I asked you for this whole tray, would you do it?"
"Yes!"
"But that would be unreasonable, wouldn't it?"
"OK! But **L**ive we always by reason NOT„ do we?"
"No! But if I asked you *'throw this whole tray to the crowd over there'* will you do it too?"

She received again an affirmative reply.

Meanwhile her friends after every patch of conversation
kept foolishly on, repeating. "Ask him! That'll show him!"

Then she did ask him! And the next thing she became aware of„ was that a few people from the crowd who had seen the gleam of cut **Diamonds**, were scrambling about on their **k**nees 'n **f**eet, while the rest just obeying a herd instinct kept joining in„ even though they didn't know what they were looking for ... Thus 'tis so„ **Self Reveals oft Human Stupidity**. The girls became afraid of the commotion„ and thinking him to be a madman edged away; and when he looked up, he found **No**where, the **f**ace that he **thought** would be **S**miling at him.

Totally Lost, closing shop„ he left fair-Grounds, to hold converse with familiar Paths 'mongst Ruins. An *Hour* deemed to pass by„ the 'most cruellest' longest *Hour* of all; when he became aware that a form had crossed him by„ and when the moon came next out of the **dark**, he was startled to find that it had been her: and thoughtlessly he traced her **s**teps. Far off ... away, on the very edge of a **darkened** **lone** Cliff ... stood a withered Tree! Up the Steep trail he saw the advancing **b**ack of her icon, which was imposed on the Skeleton of the withered Tree seeming like a huge **leaf**, whose chlorophyll sap has been eroded by some acid to leave behind an intricate net of stiff villi. The moon sporadically struggled out from behind its cover of **clouds**, to **platinise** each individual Hogweed-like **branch** of this exaggerated framework„ and thus emphasize the disparity of her **darkened** **SHADE**, whose double fell on the Ground to fold up and stain a portion of the wall-like Cliff behind. Under this fading **LIGHT**, each separate Stone cast its own penumbræ and added to the montane **S**ilhouettes a **Dimension** third. Everything absolutely was still, to give birth to an atmosphere of **G**hastly quietness„ an atmosphere of an invisible **deity**, passing its **h**ands in a slow **Rhythm** of **Waves**, over an imaginary keyboard of **blacks** 'n of whites. In the distance he saw the **Lacustrine Waters** where the moon-glade lingered„ and **thought** that were all the scintillating **ripples** of **sand**, they would appear like a texture of **s**kin on the inside of his **e**lbow: mis**F**ortune awakens the genius into a reverie, which brushes past reality to review the turmoil of **Mind**, as if magnified from afar. So everything started to withdraw at distance ... reculating towards a grand separate„ and he *felt puzzled that whenever one wanted to, one could never retrace in any of one's dreams, any of the **f**aces of one's most **Loved** ones.* His this **Brain-S**torm was jeopardized into a single orbit, by one who never had he met in any of his dream afore, though always he had had undefined longings before„ and wondered why he could never think of her except in contrast with or to, some relative surroundings ... *Objects become meaningless in isolation„ as their existence seems to be, anchored firmly into a volatile state of **Mind**:*

thus only a contradictory atmosphere can lend to Life it's Complexity and Reality.

As she had turned the corner, he couldn't see her **SHADE** any longer: so he fastened his pace, but didn't seem to be making any progress„ like a film run backwards, farther away from its object than ever. The Steep kept on passing„ the objects farther seemed moving all along with him with a strange rotatory motion in the middle„ and everything cut a semi-circle when he crossed the bend: then all the **Lighter** **S**ilhouettes of the **darker** Mountains seemed just to flit 'n flatter about in the **Sky**, along-with the movement of his **e**yes. *In depressions, one discovers that everyday **Beauty** which one never notices otherwise.* And **thought** he; how remarkable **Nature** was: little scenes expanded to whole panoramas, are always artistically balanced ... **Sometimes** cruel, and very a very often ***Beautiful***, but always pleasant: **for cruelty from the *Beautiful*„ endured is ever, with even Pleasure**.

While the Mountains rose, so high above all!

Lofty **S**ilent, aloof! And suffused with enchantment! On their regal slopes carved by the **faithless Winds„ nay faithful ... for faithless to one is, 'cause faithful to another**„ of the multi-sum of dramas of **L**ives, of so many men 'n of women, 'n of the many a many years 'fore these men 'n women were born: revealing not these secrets„ *while man the inquisitive **Beast** lurks guiltily near the fair **b**osom of **Nature**!*

Startled he realised, that she was rounding already the foot of the bridge below and hurried down. When he came to the bridge, he started to stay on even planks and kept avoiding the odd cracks„ with a strange feeling, that if he stepped even once on an odd crack, he would have to encounter great disasters. That so unreasonable an inhibition, 'twas just … that which lie in„ in the fantastic mental make-up of many a normal person. But so-on he came to a plank, which evenly was split across into two„ and due to the great caution exerted, oddly by error his fo-ot cut it. Then quite unreasonably, he started to step on the cracks and pass over the planks: until he overto-ok her„ 'n spoke breathlessly …

"Think of me as a madman **not**„ for have I a reason to speak. On first sight„ I felt I had known you of more than hundreds of thousands of years and could **L**ive the rest of my **L**ife in the limpid of your **e**yes: that when we part, the hanging images fall apart in lingering *Tear*-lets in the very closing of your **e**yes, scattering the fragments of my **Soul** along with them, to the four corners of extended **Earth**."

'Twas the moment, that the basket she had been carrying fell from her grasp„ and in the glo-omy Dimness, they saw it caught just between two Sharp Rocks right below. With a sob, she said that it contained her mother's earnings. So, he volunteered to get it for her … "**O**, but could you!"

"***Only if you ask me*** to! I am but a po-or man and have **N**othing to offer except what I am and all that I have to say to you. **Let it be the Citadel of my Love**." "**O**, please do!"

And he wondered why in moments of high seriousness, such an unconnected lot of many so a diverse event occurred … Then he asked her to give a frank reply …

"But tell me one thing? Were I to pledge you my unDying devotion, would you **Love** me?"

There she told him all … Her father had Died recently: she was left not only without protection, but without fo-od, without guidance. And she was forced to accept an old one, **to merry or not to marry**, to do or not to do„ *as per the dictates of cruel* **S**ociety*, which protects the unprotected* ***not***.

And his 'o sight a-fell„ *below* **deep** down↔down **deep** *below*„ fell a-sight 'o his. **And** on the profound **Reflections** in the **Sky** *above* which seemed like an immense **Glittering** vault of **Steel** with no redeeming features„ except the half-patch of the mo-on-**glow**. 'Twas now that her **W**ords "May **God** be with you" reached him out of an Abyss, thus detonating the whole entire of his being„ and surprise as that of a deaf man caught unwarily between a collision of speeding cars, flushed right through the totality of his existence …

"**Ô God**, **Ô God**, **Ô God**; **Ô** What's **God**? Just an image, a shape, a misty mist in short, *a* ***Nothing***, *Abstractions 'pon the* Waters *of strange floating* ***Worlds*** *of* ***thoughts****, by a smallest* Disturbance *Shattered to small* ***Nothings***! **God** is the quintessence of men's **thoughts**„ symbolizing in perfection, all qualities which lie inherent in **Nature**: man can only see this far„ **'Tis** can see Everywhere and into Everything; man has only a limited power„ **'Tis** is Omnipotent and Passes Beyond the Bonds of the Finite; remove the **L**imitations of a man and it can seem to be a **god**. *Thus each man needs a personal protector*„ who out of this vastly vast **Universe**, will remember his every little insignificant act, to weave it to **Peace** 'n **Harmony** in one **D**estiny. *Just ask how many have peopled this* ***World*** *'n you'll find no two gods ever the same!* Man is weak but has to depend on himself„ pitted against undefined forces he tries to make the odds to evens, till Death levels man's assurance: and the **Idea** of **God** was Born, 'Cause man *Dies* „ **so a** ⁋¶ystery is **solved by another** ⁋¶ystery! But **God** was never forced to **L**ive our single **L**ife„ and apparently ***seems to ignore*** all troubles wrecked on intentions of well-meaning, or of the weak.

***Human** Life is a mosaïc fragmented from slivers of Hope and Despair„* but has God ever plumbed with bleeding **f**ingers of the Despair of having all Hope Lost! And **'Tis** is Content in **'Tis** Heaven; but has **'Tis** ever Borne the *Pangs* of Starvation or the Stark Fear of Dying! Or has **'Tis** ever Longed for the Promised **Happiness**, After an Eternity of Suffering, which some God **'Tis**, beyond **'Tis** may Hold out to **'Tis**! **They say … only Misery Earns Happiness**: *Seems, God has never been embossed by **Misery**„* and seems not a fit God to rule us: **at least Not in our belittled Image of 'Tis, in our own belittled self**." *Uncertainties thrive somnabulently, up till comes a **dark** day, when a jolting accident, violently awakens them into a certain stark direction, unknown.*

Mass cords pounded on his **thoughts** and below he saw the raging torrent. He did not know how to swim, but suddenly he dived and the heavy bridge swayed ominously„ a last sentence running like a thread through an imbroglio of **thoughts**, compassed his being … "***Cut Not the Planks„ that Disaster mayn't issue***!"

*"Only those who are **alone** in Suffering realise, **True or UnTrue**, how unjust God is?"*

He hit the surface flat and Lost consciousness: all efforts at **L**ife becoming futile, because **his Feelings were too sincere to sustain a lone place in this lone World**. ***And all became darkness and rest:*** in a confusion of **R**eality and dream; in an aching existence where all Hope had been quenched by the question that *where do the millions of impossible aspirations of every single one of* **'uncounta-billions'** *of conflicting beings go,* when the vitality is sucked away: both have a **L**ife, a substance, a meaning, and both must forever remain united„ **for it seems vain to think that, after Death we become super-Human and lose all our frustrated ambitions.** He bobbed along to be soaked up in the elements to become a part of the **W**ind 'n the Water, enhancing their style 'n **Rhythm**: with his **Soul** added to the **Ocean**, the cradle of **L**ife from whose **b**osom the ardent **Vapours** part to wage war against so many unsurmountable ranges … stolid like the impassive barriers of **L**ife, defeating the ideology constituting a **Human Spirit**„ that ***burning** so in shame the humiliated clouds consume themselves in Tears of rain, to nourish the Flora with their* bl-o-od„ **biered on the silts of Rivers, to go back to their ageless mother: with these old Ideas, in time to give new births to old 'n new combinations**!

Against the ho-od of the **Sky** on the wo-oden bridge above, only one figure remained alert with one **h**and drawn back to stifle an involuntary gasp. It was that of the maiden's, who yet strove to maturity„ a still study of concern: **woman-ho-od becomes more becoming in distress**. Anxiously she waited, but **W**ords cannot whistle or gush the mounting of pressures within her. Her solitary care being the lasting sacrifice, of a **Some**one, a **Somebody** who had suddenly come to mean so much to her„ gaining to be a **Some**one … and had one analysed her mental state, this prayer would have been found 'pon her willowed **L**ips:

*"How I wish I had no **F**eelings for then I'll feel no Hurt no pain no Sadness."*

Worth is realized only when the bound binding links are disconnected:

that's why Lovers have misunderstandings … to grow more 'n more, fond of each other!

But what if the chains are Lacerated never to be re-catenæted together! She lo-oked at the frenzied swirls intermixing gashed hollow sounds 'n **Sights**, with a rise and a fall in the **Rhythm of Life**„ then heaved herself, far o'er the hanging rope railing. There was another splash and another **S**ilence. Her struggle to free his wedged **b**ody was rewarded by a quick ducking. And both Locked Together, **Never Rose-up off Death's Embrace**.

Tragedy must ensue Somehow when akin Minds fail to meet.

The moon vanished again behind its heavy lids of clouds„ and the remaining phosphorescent glow, tinctured the shapely landscape into a phantasmagoria of unmoved spectators„ printing in the lap of the **rolling** Waters the Ghostly greyness of the Negative air against the Lighter Eastern back-Ground captive, of stable **sable** peaks rising in all dire Dimensions. Only a chant of a Stray nightingale lamented their Sadness 'n their solitude united, with a sub-tryst series of thirds of softened wood-notes. **Intense** Beauty **seems** Emotion**less**: but she had Lived long enough to grasp the fact that our existence is buoyed only onto a few unexplained Values 'n unexplained spectres„ and once their vitality seeps out of the mortal chinky container, *Life is no longer worth Living„ as a cracked jar is worth mending, for it can never again hold the exact same fluids.*

What men feel sincerely remains permanent never to Die, because it forms the basis of Values 'n Ideas, which raise Life from slush 'n make it **Something** worth fighting for; even though to lose all in its ends.

And thus **A Rhythm of Two Minds** was diffused in the atmosphere to fortuitously end it„

the Life of those who meant never any Harm, but were still stamped under the shod heal of Fortune.

And Forever, in a State of Continuous Now„
In a land of dreams where Time and Space do not matter„
Their names yet are sung to ℙ¶us♪c: and their Remembrance
Lives yet in that land of dreams, attained ne'er is in distance
In Real Life„ a land where the distant Hills seem as blurred
By the mists of milky–**blue** moon-beams all spread around
To be diffused distilled, into a quiet and clearer fore-Ground.

And the ballads sing ... **that in our** sleep **we see them**
Sit nearby a running brook which murmurs simple ℙ¶us♪c
And slips thorough an arch in the woods which spans into
A small grassy stretch, thus abounding in lady's-smock„
And bound by a prim Hedge where the frolicsome gay
Butterflies rest in their drowsy moods: they live here,
On a side inside the Hedge against a mound of Rocks
In a cottage built o' bamboo shoots 'n palm leaves lone,
Bathed: in many a blue LIGHT of many a Truly True Tone.

Happened this may have not„ but when I go out alone
In the tranquil **Night**, I see the tall Trees throwing
Nigricant patches irregularly trying ... O Alas ...
To blot up scattered moon-LIGHT on untrodden grass;
And in the midst ... of this so golden Autumnal tapestry
I feel the Shades to move and I hear the stillness of ℙ¶ystery
Soft whispers whispering: to my Mind's Rhythm ... **an untold story of Love.** ... **QED** ... **End**.

10. Lahore: Punjab — ART for SENSE (How to Write?) (1957 - 15 years Jan.)

... https://pixabay.com/ ... pexels-photo-962312.jpeg ... pexels-photo-1020478.jpeg ... pexels-photo-1270184.jpeg ...

Art for art's sake, a slogan translated from the French dictum **l'Art pour l'Art**, coined in the early 19th. century by the French philosopher **Victor Cousin ...** Phrase expressing a belief held by 19th. Century writers and artists, associated with **Aestheticism**, including **Oscar Wilde**, who held that Art or Artistic Expression needs No Justification: neither that it needed to serve **Political Didactics** ... or any other Ends.

I Disagree Completely: my moto's **Logical** ... **Art for Sense**!

Every word you write must be imbibed in Thousands of years of History.
If you write something, put it away in a drawer for 25 years, when you take it out after this while and you still find it good, then it might have some value in it ... T.S. Eliot (from memory)
Drank coffee and sat for an hour. (Wastage of Civilisation, by 1st. World War) **Wasteland**
Raindrops were falling, pittery pittery pittery pat ... Sound & Sight united ... T.S. Eliot. Coined English!

... https://pixabay.com/photos/taj-mahal-sunset-taj-mahal-india-4808227/ ... taj-mahal-sunset-4808227_960_720.jpg ...
... https://pixabay.com/ ... pexels-photo-1038935.jpeg (Infinity Road) ... pexels-photo-1210273.jpeg (Heart Breaks) ...

10. Lahore: Punjab ART for SENSE (How to Write?) (1957 - 15 years Jan.)

10. Lahore : Punjab **ART for SENSE** (How to Write?) (**15 years - 1957** Jan.)

(Contradiction of ... "**Art for Arts' Sake**")

Strange **False** Theory adopted by Oscar Wilde

Children of the Night ... **OR** ... **How to Write ?**

... **In the Night of** Despair, I lay with **Misery**„ and these are my **Children Born to Me** ...

but when I had reached those cross-roads, where one realises, that **L**ife is full of a **deal** of **Ideals**, which must remain unfulfilled„ because **F**ate **renders F**atal **Blows to the Dreams of L**ife„ so be it. And then comes a time, when the last **Hop**e also ***Breaks***, having ***Broken*** all the rest ...

The Castel of ***Hop****es is Erected a Thousand Once„ to fall to* ***Ruins*** *to the* **Sands** *of* ***T****ime*„ so be it.

... I do not know what I have written„ nor do I know why have I done so ...

but I do know where to look for, while **W**riting! *A* **Candle** ***burns in LIGHT*** *and the* **Smoke** *goes unnoticed*„ like an artist who **Waters** his **Creations**, from the bleeding in the intern of his heart„ so be it. ***Every act bears two facets*** ... and what nurtures one starves the other„ so **I tried to sketch the** Smoke **behind the scorching burns of L**ife: it has remained a very elusive task„ for though the days are constantly repeated 'n numbered ...

they bring never back, the Feelings **associated to each passing** ***H****our*„ so be it.

... In my distorted Vision of **L**ife, the base of all **F**eelings is held in primary importance ...

but these **F**eelings **L**ive evanescently„ and only evanescently can they be caught! *Such* ***S****entiments and* ***E****motions ... have to be coaxed 'n caressed* ***L****ovingly near oneself„ because like innocent 'n delicate children, they'll succumb to a hostile gaze*„ so be it. So, my digressions are ***a tentative experiment in abstract in the dark***„

in an effort, to recreate the **Beauty** 'n **Rhythm** of **Art** ... of what are capable„ my simple wits„ so be it.

... I've written much about **L**ove: where, often I have employed multiple images ...

but these can also be regarded to have been in use since centuries 'n centuries„ so be it ! 'Twas NOT for adornment, or due to an 'imagination lack'„ so be it ! **'Twas done to try to assemble concepts** ...

a relationship of elements„ *the permanent in the material, to the permanent in the* ***Ideal***„ so be it !

Love like Beauty, is Linked to the Universe„ for it is as Old as the Stars„ so be it !

... *Imitations NEVER can be cut to* ***Diamonds*** ...

but What is, **IS** ... so„ even in the effort to regulate the old images to my new requirements, I have tried my best to remain original: for **Originality is the Theme of Creation**„ so be it ! Furthermore, every single letter has **W**ritten itself spontaneously„ while the whole is composed of a cautious '**Idea**' prunation ...

for Detail is the Medium of Art„ as In-opionation is its Soul„ so be it **...**

I must apologise for one thing though. I consider the gap between the **comma** (,) and **semi-colon** (;) to be too Sharp and Steep„ ***so be it***. Thus, I have developed a **New Stoppage**„ which I propose to call the '**pause**' („)„ ***so be it***. Often, these '**pause**' signs are used as regards rests and/or inflections„ rather than as any formal *Breakage* between any clauses or having any great complexities of grammar: a sort of an ***intake of breath***„ like in the **theatre dialogues**, or acts, or scenes„ ***so be it***„ if you will„

just call it my innovative idiosyncrasy„ if you really will„ will„ will„ „ „ „ ***so be it***„

I am not a native born to this language„ but I sincerely Hope that my transgressions will be excused as un**pardon**able as **pardon**able„ and will not be subjected to the rigours of a dis-jointing 'post-mortem'. Ernest '**Critics**' devoid of feeling, conduct a *Painful* '**Autopsy**' on a **L**iving work of imagination„ ***so be it***„ and quash the moving **Spirit** within„ reducing it to a state of 'still-mate', thus a still-born„ 'of rigor-mortis'„ giving **Truth** to ... till 'Death' do us 'part' ... or 'apart' ... as the case may be ? **Long L**ive **'**Dead **Critics' !**

Oh ... so finally, **my Only Wish is**„ ***so be it***„ ...

- **o**ft that I be exempted with grace„
- **o**f being labelled with any **F**alse **Ideas**„
- **o**f which I never may have ever dreamt„
- **o**f even in the **W**ildest of my **W**ild dreams„
- **o**nly preferring 'n praying, that if you like me„
- **o** let me live in the deep interior of your hearts„
- **o**r, if you do not, then let me Die in the obscurity„
- **o**y an impractical person, ô thinking too too much„
- **o**verall, who once so squandered all„ above and overall„
- **o**ften all letting go Waste„ 'n in **L**ife„ 'n in **T**ime„ 'n in **S**pace„
- **o**r in **dark thoughts**„ 'n in deep pensive mood„ 'n pensive grace„
- **o**r t'riddling quietly by„ ever softly by„ at a slowly lumbering pace„ ***so be it***„ ...

10. Marseille **MA Si BELLE MÈRE** — **My So Strong a Mom** 1982

Mon fils si tu parles
C'est une Rayure
Sur une Pierre
Qui une Éternité éternité demeure
Donc tu veilleras sur tes mots.

Toute ta **V**ie mon fils
Tu surveilleras tes actes
Ne salis pas ton proche
Ni tes aïeux ni ton être
Le respect de ton être
Tu le tiens
Dans tes mains
Et tu le sauveras mon cher fils
Le meilleur respect de toi-même
Est le respect des autres.

Et mon fils tu seras fier
De ton être et ton Sort
Puis tu aideras tant de gens
Ils te feront bien du *Mal*
Et tu Souris quand je parle
Mais tes actes sont pour toi
N'oublies pas que dans ce **Monde**
Tu as à solder tous tes comptes.

Ces cinq lettres qui font **Amour**
Tu les trouveras bien plus tard
Quand le temps sera mûr
Et ton sang sera pur
Tu pourras **Aimer** donc une femme
à la hauteur de ton **Âme**
En **Amour** tu donnes ton Cœur
Ne cherchant jamais le retour
Seul le Destin fait le tour
Tu vaudras ce que tu voudras toujours.

My son if you speak
'Tis a soft Stripe
On soft Rock
That an Eternity stays
So'll care about your words.

All your **L**ife my son
You'll control your acts
Don't dirty your nears
Nor yourself nor your sears
The respect of your being
You hold it
In your hands
And you'll know my dear son
The best respect of yourself
Is in respecting all others.

And my son you'll be proud
Of your-self 'n your Sort
So you'll aid many a folk
They will *Hurt* you at their will
And you Smile when I speak
But your acts are for you
Forget not that in this **World**
You must balance all accounts.

These four letters writ as **Love**
You'll find much too late
As your times will mature 'n wait
And your blood'll be purèd
Only then you'd **Love** a maid
At the height of your **Soul** so made
In **Love** you give your heart
Never hoping a return
Only Destiny can oe'r-turn
You'll be worth your want as worth.

(**10th. anniversary of her** Death ... hoping to have deceived her never ever.
Why is nature so economic 'n close-fisted on such persons?)
A true Impératrice of the Heart ... **Méraj Suharwardi Hameed** ...

ext. **French.** ***thBk-F-3.pdf*** ... *Ma Si Belle Mère* 1982 p-14--64--**248**-

Simples sont les règles de ce **Monde**
Mais moins simple est de les pratiquer
Avec grandeur et honnêteté
Tu suivras ton bon sens
Et tu feras ce que tu penses
Souviens-toi de ce que je dis
Même s'il te paraît inédit
" **les plus proches font plus *Mal***
de plus loin
que les éloignés
de plus près. "

Et mon fils quand tu seras grand
Tu comprendras ce que je dis
Je suis peut-être une vieille **V**ie
Mais les **Souvenirs** sont bons
Quand les aimés s'en vont.

Elle me manqué cette mère
Qui m'a porté de mon père
Qui m'a fait **si vieux si jeune**
Elle est Morte et puis encore
Aussi vieille que les siècles
Mais qui veille d'une bonne mine
Que ces vieilleries qu'elle m'a apprises
Ne vieillissent jamais depuis
Des vieux débuts
Des vieux temps des vieilles gens.

Maintenant **tariq** est si grand
Et son être est son maître
Peu de choses
Font un peu le tracé de sa **V**ie
Peu de paroles d'une grande dame
Peu de fierté et d'**Amour**
Et le respect de tout
Et le peu qui l'entoure.

Simple are the rules of this **World**
But less simple is how to practice 'em
With grandeur 'n honesty
You'll follow your good sense
And you'll do the best what seems
Remember ever what I say
Even if appears it out of the way
" **the most near make more *Hurt***
from more far
than the further
from more near. "

And my son when you'll be grown
You'll capt what I said
Am perhaps an old **L**ife in bed
But **Souvenirs** are only good
When the **L**ovéd become Dead wood.

I miss this ma
Who me ported off my pa
Who made me **so old so young**
She's Dead 'n then again
As old as the begin
But who looks on of a good mien
That these oldnesses me she taught
Come never old as brought
Since such an ancient start
Of older times of older guard.

Now **tariq** is so grand
And his self is his sage
Lil so little a thing
Trace the curve of his **L**ife
Lil bit of words of a grand'dame
Lil bit of honour 'n of **Love**
An' the respect of all
An' a lil bit all around at fall.

(Le **10ième. anniversaire de sa mort** ... j'espère ne l'avoir déçu jamais.
Pourquoi est la nature si économe et avare de telles personnes ?)
Une Impératrice du Cœur ... **Méraj Suharwardi Hameed** ...

11. Marseille **MON Si BON PÈRE** — **My So Good a Papa** 1982

Père

comme c'est réconfortant
de vous tenir le **d**oigt
mais dans quelques **T**emps
où seras-tu toi ?

Père

pourquoi aidez-vous
tous ces gens
qui en leur bon moment
t'oublient
subitement ?

Fils

je donne toi et leurs ce que j'ai
et puis
quelle autre raison d'être
ai-je ?

Père

je vous comprends
le refus du **Mal**
est devenir grand
des deux grandeurs
du **c**orps et de l'**Âme**
d'accord
pour une fois
je donne l'autre **j**oue
mais explique moi
ce que tu feras
si on te frappe
encore et encore sur cela ?

Fils

si tu peux emporter
au-delà
de ce **Monde**
cette **j**oue
" **frappe** "
mais apprends
à laisser déjà
ce que tu dois laisser
ici

Pa

so recomforting 'tis
to see you hold my **h**and
but after some **T**ime
where will you be ?

Pa

why do you help
all 'n the sundry
who in their good moments
forget it
suddenly ?

Son

give thou 'n them I what can I
'n then
what other reason to be
have I ?

Pa

understand you I
refusing **Evil**
is becoming great
of this pair in greatness
of **c**orpse 'n of **Soul**
so ok
for once
give I the other **c**heek
but explain me
what will you do
if one slaps you
on this one again 'n again ?

Son

if you can export
unto the beyond
of this **World**
this **c**heek
" **hit** "
but learn
already to abandon
what must you abandon
here

quand le **T**onnerre
de ce **Monde**
aura **é**claté
puis dans tes débris
est-ce que tu auras
ailleurs d'autres biens
que tes pensées autres ?

Père

comme c'est réconfortant
de vous tenir le **d**oigt
mais **père**
promettez-moi
quand le **Mal** de ce **Monde**
m'envahira
tu viendras me voir
ne penses-tu pas
je serais perdu sans toi ?

Fils

je ne suis qu'une pensée
je te donne ce que j'ai
puis t'es seul
tout est **seul**
ainsi est la loi
de ce **Monde**
mais n'oublie pas
que ton **Âme** est la seule ta voie
même Devin s'oblige
de te la laisser n'est-ce pas ?
et **fils** je t'
embrasse cette dernière fois
maintenant va jouer
dans les Jardins **E**pineux de ce **Monde**
ce n'est qu'un aspect du **Paradis** **P**erdu
et quand on se retrouvera
dans l'au-delà
on rira de tout cela … n'est-ce pas ?

when the **T**hunder
of this **World**
will **b**urst
then in your rubble
'twould remain
elsewhere other goods
than your other thinks ?

Pa

so re-comforting 'tis
to see you hold my **h**and
but **pa**
promise me
when the **Evil** of this **World**
will attack me
come'll you to me to see
don't you think
lost'll be I without thee ?

Son

am I not but a thought
give U I what have I
then U'r lone
all r **alone**
so is the law
of this **World**
but forget it not
that your **Soul** is Ur sole way
even Devine does self-restrict
to leave it U na ?
'n **son** I U
embrasse this last day
go now to play
in the **T**horny Gardens of this **World**
'tis but an aspect of the **Paradise** **L**ost
'n when we'll reunite
in the yond
one'll laugh afore beyond … na ?

… **16 janvier 1982** … Un Impérateur du Cœur … **Khan Sahib Mian Abdul Hameed** … Emperor of Hearts …
un quart de siècle aujourd'hui qu'il n'est plus là, mais ses paroles résonnent toujours, en tête et autours !
a quarter century today that he's no more here, but his words resound always, in head 'n surround !

ext. **French.** ***thBk-F-3.pdf*** … *Mon Si Bon Père* 1982 p-17--67--251-

9. .Paris. **Mon ANCIEN Serviteur** **My ANCIENT Servitor** 1980

quand je serai Mort mon fils
tu m'enterreras sous un arbre
sous l'**O**mbre d'un arbre
c'était un être
très très simple
un grand maître plus grand que d'autres
il m'a raconté des histories
de ' ici et là-bas '
de ce qui était et n'était pas
mon fils tu seras le poète
de la ***D**ouleur* et de l'**Amour**
je t'apprendrai tant de choses
sur ce qui est ta cause
la ***D**ouleur* de l'**Amour**
de la finesse de la **V**ie
des **l**armes des gens
qui ont souffert dans le **T**emps
mais mon fils quand je serai Mort
tu m'enterreras comme je dors
sous l'**O**mbre d'un arbre
il était un être très très simple
un grand maître plus grand que d'autres
mon ancien serviteur
et quand j'enterre mon **Âme**
dans un soufflé très calme
sous l'ombre d'un arbre
je pense à cet être
mon ancien serviteur
enterré sous les **Ombres**
d'un arbre qui pleure
et son **tariq** qui chante
et les Oiseaux l'écoutent

when I'll Die my son
do bury me under a tree in Thorn
in the **S**hadows of its borne
'twas a person
so so simple
so great a master the greatest of all
he recounted me stories
of ' where 'n there '
of what came to pass 'n what did not
my son you'll be the poët
of ***P**ain* 'n of **L**ove
then I'll tell you many so a tale
of the brunt of your cause
of the ***P**ain* of **L**ove
of the fineness of **L**ife
of the **t**ears of the gents
who have suffered in the **T**imes
but my son when I'll Die
you'll bury me as I dose
in the **S**hadow of its borne
'twas a person so so simple
so great a master the greatest of all
my ancient servitor
'n when I bury my **Soul**
in a wisp so calm
in the **S**hadow of a palm
thinking 'twas he a psalm
my ancient servitor
buried in the **Shades**
of trees which weep
'n his **tariq** who chants
'n Birds listen to sleep

Maître Ashraf : Qui m'avait élevé depuis bébé ... [20 ans] Son Conte de Fée Continue Encore ...
Master Ashraf : Who brought me up since child ... [20 years] His Fairy Story Still Continues ...

ext. **French.** ***thBk-F-3.pdf*** ... *Mon Ancien Serviteur* 1982 p-13--63--247-

a half century today that he's no more here, but his words resound always, in heads 'n surrounds !

11. Lahore : Punjab **That Day My Father Died** **2007** (65 years)

16/01/**1948**	He had 9 years	Brother's Birthday
16/01/1957	**(My 15th. year)**	**Writ: 15/01/2007**
16/01/1978	**(My 36th. year)**	French Nationality

Dear, Dr. **Azam** Chaudhry (Sorbonne .Paris.) *Friend of Long Date*

For … My Sis & Bro. … & All Family Friend … ***& in the Memory of Ammi***

To Wish to All of You … My Best of Best Wishes.

Morrow is **16/01/2007** … **50** years past, on same, my Father Breathed his Last; while Innocent Brother Dear of 9 … Danced and Clapped his **H**ands for a Merited Birthday Present.

… He Got NONE …

In the Same Home, exact 15 days later (31st.) … did Die Uncle … also named same.

Abdul Hameed, father of Sultan "**Chotay**" Bhai. Since so 50 years, I fest NONE 16th Jan. Elders gone, Family destroyed, I so became an Elder Young King … for over a 3rd Century … waiting that youngs' take over … Since then, I have **0** & I will have **0** … 'Tis My Single Rule of **L**ife … Be it clearly understood. Today, I pass **lone**, this day **alone**, all **alone** … **for it starts me to THINK.**

What is Life & What is Death …

What is Dream & What is Reality …

What is True & What is False …

What is Reverie & What is a Lie …

Where's a Divide? Compromise? Confession?

(or Christianity … or Islamic … or TAUBA …)?

I I I have found NONE … Have U U U?

But What I I I have only found is …

"I Confess that I am FALSE … I a Liar."

And now, allow me to explain U the Why … of the Whole …

Gents came from far all gay, with a **L**augh & a **J**oke.

They knew not that … the Young at the door, was the Elder's Son.

10 Meters away, they put a VEIL on their NOSE, to HIDE their SHAME,

& Burst Out in TEARS, a **C**ry 'n BLOOD 'n **SAND**, replacing Ho Ho Ha Ha Hi Hi.

In 1 ***Hour*****Ssss**, **I Learnt a World** a 100 **T**ime**Ssss**: **& Hypocrite am I, I; & I for ever'rrrr.**

r u also? Ô, a Bit? **NOooo**! So Let US **L**augh & **S**mile & do a *quick* **Quick-Step**, Yester & Now & Morrow. And please, on the 27th. of **01 January 2007**, will start an Islamic year with **Muharram** … which was always surely APT for SACRIFICES: **Let Us Unite to Divide** … U & Me & b = V. Promise ???

-Iqbal- **" Mullah** ki Azan aur hai, **Mujahid** ki Azan aur? **"** … Let's b FRANK: **True** or **F**alse?

Then if I CONFESS … WHO 2 CONFESS 2 ? WHO 2, U **U** U or Mi **Mi** Mi ? Hi **Hi** Hi ?

CONFESS or TAUBA ? Which ??? My EXCUSES !!! **Ô** Dear DEAR Friends !!!

It's with a SOFT Heart, that I write this 2-day !!! (a bit distorted) 2 Alll !!!

& So Let us call all **Mi Evil** … as THOUGHTS just FLY away …

*** **To Get POWER … We Can Even Pose as MUSLIMS** *** ***(Unknown)*** Hi Hi ?

12. Lahore : Punjab **Hut on the Hill** 1/10 (**1957** - 15 years Jan.)

At Dawn *Break*, a happy twinkling morning Star had brought tidings of the blushing Sun, and so had made a graceful exit; fading out as the end ripple fades on the surface of the calm Waters flirted by,, bye the Lightest breath of air: just a dim image of the Sunrise Reflected in the whitening Sky,, and this widening circle, that spread from the ¶¶ystery East, assured that the Steel-grey Mountains shook away their quiet gravity, to reassume the joyous green of the undergrowth, speckled with the slaty brown of the Rocks strewed ***about***.

The Sun arose,, to fix a hovering **e**ye o'er the landscape, of pellucid air with pure *Sparkles* clear,, which so was washed clean of all impurities of **Worldly** Dust: bathing even the minutest **Earthy** Particle in its golden Rays,, except where the giant Pine Trees outlined an irregular Shadow, filtering the **Sky** ***above***.

The far-off chumps of sparse Trees were half-enveloped in rising mists of melting dews,, and against such a **darker** back-Ground of sombre penumbræ Silhouettes, the country-scope sloped gently up, to end in a level stretch, where stood a log cabin. 'Twas a **hexagonal** Hut,, a six sided **filled Universe** … behind old oldened, wooden a Hut-ty,, where Pine Trees rose to dizzy heights on the still endlessly rising slope, curtaining the distant peaks, away so far ***away***,, lost to view.

Ages ago, looming large out of the past **black** pitched **Night**,, this dilapidated structure confronted all alone, tired **thoughts** so full of Emotions,, these Emotions repeating the same **W**ords of ages bygone, echoing persistently still, from the folds of older **M**emories,, like distorted husky **whispers** engulfing a **Night**-mare ***near***.

Then a few falling leaves settled like locust swarms on the quietly resting Trees,, till a gust of **W**ind makes them fly and strinkling the amber **Earth** with a carpet of lemon 'n brown orange woven from the wrinkles of **camel** tint Paper, tinged all over of **red** spots, in its ambary folds ***below***.

Then on felt a Tremor

… Fear … Danger … Death …
seemed to lurk,, waiting 'n awaiting; in the **dark darknesses dark**,,
of folds and folds of **ravaged times**,,
of the **haunted** house ahead,,
… old old old … cold cold cold …

Thus trembling, I woke up … **perchance 'twas it a dream** ?

… And that dream happened,, so multiple a times …

… And then went away … for a **long longer** while … to ***come*** … or to ***go*** …

(*Now I open a parenthesis*)

(… … … This is a story of the 'good' of 'Knowledge' and the '**Evil**' of 'Ignorance',, and of a **How** ? **How** all can be destroyed by '**prejudice**' …

"**The greater the religious fervour, the filthier the Mind**,, because in principle, the origin of religion is a check on base '***Passions***',, but those who act 'pious', feel urged by their nagging '**Desires**' inside,, undermining this check of **Fears**, in the form of 'traditions',, thus probing the secrets of others, in inside of themselves to substantiate their own 'undress' of '**Evil**',, for feeling themselves to be 'naked', thus wanting to see the others 'naked' also,, replaced into their own place! Thus the 'selfish', impose the 'guilt' of their **Evil** 'conscious',, sallying the 'goodwill' of the 'others' so 'pure'. An example is … where certain old women often sort out, or 'feign' of 'chastity' as a 'pretext',, then go away in 'groups', to 'gossip' about each other,, all '**Dust**' and '**Dirt**'. Just ask honestly, so thou wilt know,, all those who 'professed' or 'preached', but how many of them can be deigned to possess '**True**' religion,, or an established '**unselfish**' and clear 'goodness' of '**heart**' …"? A Perfect '**Catharsis**' ?

Thus steams our story of '**D**estruction **by Ignorance**' … … …**)**

(*Parenthesis Now thus closed*)

* * * * * * * * *

[[[… Here I stopped … 50 years topped …
for I know **N**othing … of **Ignorance**
thus learnt I long … a **L**ife-time along
to re-learn the **Knowledge** … of **Ignorance D**estructed
but how to maintain … far away in will
the neat pure innocence … of a sweet sweeter child … **]]]**

My **Love** asked me, "But I know **N**othing of you?" So I said, "We'll **see**, we'll **see**, I promise we'll **see**." **The WHY**!

* * * * * * * * *

… The '**essence of L**ife' so '**relates**' many much many '**cross stories**' at the '**same physical time**' …

[[[… **So as has become our habit … we open again a parenthesis** … **]]]**

… 'Twas a **hexagonal** hut,, a six sided **filled Universe** …

('Tis a **story** of **two** events separated,
related 'n **unrelated**,,
the '**action**' of the '**normal**',
'n the '**reaction**' of the '**calculated**',,
of how all can be '**corrupted**',
by '**disintegrity**',, inborn**)**

12. Hut on the Hill 2007 (55 years Jan.) **Fifty years had passed** 3/10

(Once it came in a Dream, on thinking ... of ... the Hut on the Hill) ... For a **Loveless** Lady !

The Goat and The Lion

"Once there **L**ived a **goat** and a **lion**. The mother **goat** had two kiddy kids, who sucked her milk„ as **Nature** willed. One day a hungry **lion** king, so thus made meal„ without making any deal. But the **lion** had forgotten, what **Grand Mother Nature** had begotten„ that his own two kiddy kids needed NO Red meat, ONLY needed they ... white milk„ ever so sweet ... Of a good heart, the **goat** so smart„ went up to the **Lion** King and said as a start, "Mr. **Lion** King: if you eat me, your **cubs** would Die of hunger„ so will it be." And **Reflecting**, then the smart **Lion** King said, "So say we, but tell me„ what can we do?" And the **goat** replied, "Let me feed them first, if you me can trust„ then we'll see?" Thus grew up the two kids, biding with wondering **L**ids„ in the Forest midst!

To Discern a Lady ... look at her Springs? If Off-Springs are **Null**, Lady's **Null**!

"They **L**oved her so much, who now became their mother-like„ and ran around her all day ever together. But **L**ife is **L**ife, so came so„ that day by day, the **Lion** King became older 'n older„ as becomes the normal **Worldly** strife. Thus he called his now grown **cubs** to say, "Honour your Mother as a Queen„ for but before soon ... 'twill come so, that I'll disappear in the green." And exactly, that's what he did„ in a teeny wean.

"The **Power Kids** then called Council. 'Go and announce to all and sundry, if be it so then go all hungry„ but touch never our Mother, never 'n never or never„ or we'll be very much very **A**ngry'. Thus Ever in the Forever, roamed she around„ all around and round, in the Vale and in the green„ and in between. But our story ends not here, not so in the unseen„ so stay with me a while more, Sire, and bear and hear.

"A **falcon** from far had seen this whole scene, so murmured to himself„ 'But? If a good **goat** can be good, so can I be good also„ that **God** be begot: Good **God**'! It was then that he saw, a **rat** drowning in the Water so raw„ far so far belooooow, deep below! With a dive and a swish, in beak and in claw„ he got the **rat** out, for he was very stout„ oh how 'n how 'n how? He brought the **rat** to his nest, doing only his best„ a **rat** who was only a tout; feeding him and kneading him„ being so **W**arming and **L**oving him! (Story of Reasoned Self-Interest)

"Once the **rat** had taken his rest and food and all that he could, he started to brood„ and changed his mood. And when the noble **falcon** went off to sleep, for so tired was he that he couldn't an **e**ye open keep„ the **mousy rat** in a single twink, clipped off the drowsy **falcon**'s wing„ so that when he woke up, to walk down or up, Rock or Pebble„ he had to crutches to cling. Matters it but NOT? **Troubles Last NOT Long ... when Dealt Well**!

"Thus from far 'n safe, the mean **Mousy rat**, on the Ground spate„ 'n then so spake, 'Mean is Mean and Dean is Dean„ *was not spoken of the **Soul***; as Dust thou art to returnest to Dust„ for ... **to Raise the Low, is the Fall of the Earnest**!' Then went he away, to drown the next day„ in the same Stream, in the same sway„ for 'twas no flying **falcon**, to help him in his dismay„ oh oh oh ... a **Mouse's a Mouse**: Wherever he may be!"

[[[... **Moral** ...]]] On where NO Honour is ... Waste NOT thy Bounty„
Dearth on **Earth** is Plenty„ **for Mean's NO Donner**.

(We close again a parenthesis)

(Once it came in a Dream, on thinking ... of ... the Hut on the Hill) ... For a **Loveless** Lady !

Aristotle and Alexander

What **matters** to '**smallness**', is the **Downfall** of **Greatness** !

[[[... **Thus as is an established our habit now, we open again another parenthesis** ...]]]

"The great Aristotle had a small student„ of the name Alexander. Once this unknown Alexander, but did fall in **Love**„ with a Clever Courtesan. Aristotle warned him, for but a small student was he„ 'be but aware: for she's but a smart and a cunning woman'. Unheeding, the Prince carried on„ but one day confided to her what the Master had said. So she planned, planning otherwise„ and became friendly with the Sage. Then she told the King, to watch from a *certain* roof-hole„ into a *certain* room, at a *certain* Time. A *certain* Alexander the Great obeyed, to lo 'n to behold„ a *certain* woman clad in inviting, entering a *certain* door„ and teasing so a *certain* Wise-man ...

'I want to ride a **horse**, ô *certain* sear'„
'But there is none here, ô *certain* dear'„
'Yes we have ... so my *certain* **horse**, be„ on all **f**eet four, be: come near'.

"As Aristotle, squatted down„ then so she hit, 'n bit 'n beat 'n whipped the Sage, for an hour or so„ and then left him, inviting him„ for **Nothing** more ... Amused the Victor, thus one day recounted to his famed teacher„ what he had seen ... then advised him, not be a preacher„ for '**She made a** bloody **fool out of You**'!

"And Aristotle, laughed out loud„ 'Son' said he, 'son I knew you were watching„ so let it be, but I wanted to teach you a **Silvered Lesson**'„ and continued ... '***Never to tread in*** *Dirty Waters*, ***where alligators may seem to be***„ let this be written in bold, for 'tis worth its weight in **Gold**„ what you must learn to hold ... then so, Ô **Mortal Prince**, for I've known you from child-hood 'n since„ **Tutor was I**, so *certain* a **Tutor I remain**!"

[[[... **Moral** ...]]] Ask not the **Sky**, to **Rats** 'n **Worms** 'n the Lowly„
Leave it to Lofty Fliers; for such Never Liars can they be.

(*Anew is closed again a parenthesis*)

... https://www.pexels.com/search/ ... crete-78954_960_720.jpg ... lion-3676984_960_720.jpg ...
... sculpture-378280_960_720.jpg (Alexandre) ... https://www.pixabay.com/photos/sculpture-art-aristotle-statue-3399968/ ...

Sa'adi Shaykh of Persia

Of **cunning** and of '**stales**', we can **Tell** many **Tales**„
Of how the **low** can '**trod**' the **High**, **ho ho**„
'n as per **last**, so '**opens**' that what **Ends**„ **the past** !

[[[... **Thus as is well established a habit now, opening at last a last parenthesis** ...]]]

"In Persia, there lived once a Sheikh„ a Sage Sheikh called Sa'adi, the Sheikh. He had written many a book, on **Poetry** 'n **Perfumes** 'n **Flowers** 'n on Gardens„ well as including many Tales, on the Cunning of Women. As he knew all about it now, he decided to sell his good books collection in the market„ that it served an else one meriting. So he loaded all these works on an Ass, that merit be and be enhanced„ and then slowly 'n steadily, **hanking his knowledge loaded ass**, to the nearest bazaar„ just walked besides it.

"Fate: be it that on his way, he met a good woman„ just walking aStray. 'How do you do, Sa'adi my good man„ what's all this that you take away, so earnestly'? 'Only books to sell out, for those who need help„ in distract or adversity'! 'Say, say, say„ aye, aye, aye„ on what Subjects, if I may'? '**On the Cunning of Women**, who can make, if need be„ an honest man sway'! 'Come, come„ know you all about it; "***of Women***": seems strange„ but I pray, O pray'? 'All, I said„ if I may ... allllll I know, you„ me, or we„ or they„ however unknown be it or they.'

" 'Ha, Ha', said the woman„ 'Pray! Shall I show you a **New Trick**' 'Pray, Nay„ Not Today'! 'Ha, Ha'„ said the woman. Then she Tore her Clothes, to start in a loud voice in a shout„ 'Hey, Hey„ Help, Help„ Hey, Hey' ... **Sa'adi** surprised was beat up by the **crowd**, hearing her voice„ so **loud**. Then elapsed a few moments, that intervened she„ in a manner very stout, still screaming ... 'Not, him„ Hey, Hey„ I Cried; Help, Sa'adi„ Help, Help. Robbers attacked me, and he came to me aid„ please Help, Sa'adi„ Hey, Hey„ **Beat him Not**, Oey„ Oey'!

" Thus, in a nearby Stream, Sa'adi threw his Knowledge loaded Books„ for he had learned, as in an Awakened Dream„ **Women's many a Trick** ... How to Fling a Man in a Flick„ in a single Eye's Blink 'n Click."

[[[... **Moral** ...]]] Madame if you liked it, condescend to be **Ma Dame**„
My Mistress: as be, but ... Not ever My Miss-**Ma-Stress**„ **Ma-Dame**.

(*Last time is closed finally our parenthesis*)

True **Happiness** ... **Delves** to Needfull! 'Tis Worth a Million **Prayers** ... or many a Million Bows to the **Sublime**: who does'nt Need them! **Sa'adi Shaykh**	The Best **L**oved by **God**, are only **Poor**! Are **Rich** as Humble as the **Poor** ... Still these **Poor**, have often the **Magnanimity**, of them called **Rich**! **Sa'adi Shaykh**	Be Aware of your **Ennemies**! And also of your **Friends** ... When start they, falsely hippocratically be, **Friends Flatters**! **Sa'adi Shaykh**	

... https://unsplash.com/photos/P_Ne56WEe5s ... photo-1554058922-d51b58b707f5.jpg (Persian Mosque) ...

12. **Hut on the Hill** **2017** (60 years Jan.) **Sixty years had passed** 6/10

For a **Lovely** Lady ... a Half being done ... a Half to do
Sixty years had now passed ... Then saw I once again in a dream
Perched on Top of the Hill, was the Hut ... A Strange **Hut**, but but but ...
Old old old, 'twas ... As saying goes: *Ruins testify„ that the **Edifice** was Magnificent* ...
Beauty's bound; to 'n unto History ... ***'n Stories take form, only when there's Mystery*** ...

The Architect was so Magnanimous, that one could Peep into the Past ... A Strange Hut Shack Hut, with Arches and Arcs ... Ô oozing forth **Perfumes**, of **Flowers** 'n Gardens 'n Parks ... All **desolate** and quiet, 'tis **Lost** Splendour bright ... Where the past sculpted wood-work, let pass a sniff 'n whiff of air ... Where now the **W**ind roared, with a ***Fury*** so rare ... That Strangers became breathless, when the curious became restless and the passers became step-less„ holding on to their mantels; of Fear of loosing 'em in an Eternity, of **Sight 'n Sound**!

Such was the Mystery 'n such were the means to comprehend it ... **Incomprehensible** ...

Hut on the Hill 12/01/**2017** **Sight 'n Sound**

'Twas with the lady I **Loved**, that I went to see again, ô years after, the **H**ut on the **H**ill ... The **first T**ime !
She had asked me, " But I know **N**othing of you ? " So I said, " We'll **see**, we'll **see**, I promise we'll **see**. "
Thus I took her out to **see**, what 'twas the **InComplete** of my **L**ife; for she there, all other was **Complete** !

'Twas a **S**tormy round; rain 'n **Water** on **G**round; 'n **W**ind blew 'n **leaves** flew; 'n the air took a **dark** a hew !
Few 'n fewer around, in this visit to astound; 'n so in past became I, **Sight 'n Sound**„ 'n so bound.
We went not inside, as was a hush to surround; we just roamed all around„ to be back for another round.
'Twas then, the **Mind** woke up, as came the bye-gones by back ... 'n so became so kiddy, she 'n I ! Aye, aye !
" When oft upon my couch I lie, in vacant or in pensive mood, they come upon the **Mind's** inner **e**ye ... "
A hoard of **golden M**emories ... these daffy daffodils ... in this Hutty on the **H**ills ... (*Wordsworth*).

Then I went back into my child-hood; for child-hood 'tis, so ***Broken***, when you leave your house, for the first **T**ime. I had left the twinkling **LIGHTS** of the **Illuminated** city, took a plane **lone** 'n lame, landing up so to say, in the glorious city of lil-lllll**London** : If it were done when 'tis done, then 'twere well It were done quickly: (Shakespeare so said ... stand I so corrected, in desperation). So this famous **Lone**-Done, gave me it's first surprise ... Used to **Rivers** 'bout a mile large 'n wide back home; and my cousin, who had come to pick me up, passed a bridge grandiosely and told me, " We're now crossing the **Thames River** ". Surprised, I muttered, " This **brook** ? " Far very Far ... from ... 'Twas a **hexagonal** hut„ a six sided **filled Universe** ...

Ô Tiny Thames, **Jeeves 'n James**, Ô Christ ... **His Cross 'twas bit thinner**, than what we'd crossed.

Anyway, we crossed, came home; 'n **Nighty** o **Nighty** ... First Tourisms done !!! So 'Lon' was 'done' 'n went off into the Past. Later came, the Second Tourism ! Hardly two months had gone by, that I came into my primary contact with the renowned global 'n glorified **Industrial Revolution**, of which we speak incessantly! If 'twere young then ('n **Hope** still living)! Recollect, the famous Lon-Done **SMOG** of 1962 (**Sm**oke + **F**o**g**) ... Five Surgical Masks on the **N**ose (fortunately, my cousin was a doctor): two months, so thick that you could not count your two **f**ingers, at an **a**rm's length; buses were closed and if ever you went out: coming back, you could not recognise your home ... my only **Recognise Point**, was a surgery in front, whose so funny a sign-board spoke for self; inscribed "**Dr.** Death": hi-hi: (fortunately, he was a Dentist; for Dead Teeth), hi-hi!

Hut on the Hill 13/01/**2017** **Souls 'n Spirits**

These were my first steps or toddles in Naked Lon-Done ... I looked for a job, which as was not so easy to find; thus I used me largely free Time to do sight-seeing in a very original manner ... but 'twould be better to say, that 'twas more the **Sights** Seeing, lil little me ... hi-hi, I'll explain ... taking a map, precisely the '**A to Z**' that then was of 120 pages, I walked about 2 pages a day; thus poor **Sights** could see me, & I them, a sort of Mutual Satisfaction ... a method radically simple„ cause I didn't want any Sight to miss me; so I started, on left at the top of the page and started to walk on the road to the right ! Right ? Come at the Road End, I descended a crank and started to walk on the next road, street, passage, alley, avenue or relatives; but this Time to the left: and so on & so forth ... so around mid-day, I had done the first page ... then a bit of a pause, a small 'casse-croûte'; a piff of Water 'n a puff of air: 'n awe, me, map 'n crap, to start a walk again ... Yo Ho 'n a bottle of mumps ... Thus 2 months went by, bye-bye; and with honour, I can affirm, that **London** can proudly assert: it's the 1st. City in this **wHole** a **World**, that's **Complete** Sight-Seen lil mi ...

Later, years after, .Paris., ***Basel*** 'n Roma suffered a same Sort ... **City Mortar's my Love**!

Finding an Article-ship was a Blow ... my toddles were trumped 'n stumped; I had seriously to work, but was fortunate in my studies, passing all eXams, at the first go ... My culture as well, was largely enhanced ... I saw **Margo** & **Nurev** together 8 times, saw '**Six Characters in Search of an Author**' of Pirandello, by an Italian Group; and '**The Rope**' of Agatha (a play that passed a third of a century on stage ... a play in which, myself I acted as a comic, in **Lahore** in 1966) ... Thus my student life was full of interest ! I even had had the honour to have audited '**Harrods**' for my Principle, where we caught a ... chuuuut ... didn't say a **W**ord !

Our **first** visit done, of "We'll **see**, we'll **see**, I promise we'll **see**." I then again took her to a 'Hut **on the** Hill'! This **second** Time there was no **T**hunder no rain, no clamour no drain ... 'Twas a sunny day and the hut seemed so cool so inviting, so calm so exciting ... looked like 'the Hut' changed moods on seeing my dear **L**ady-**L**ove, to show **Something** different 'n diverse; 'n concerning the normal, all inverse; all reverse ...

Inside, there was no hew nor **C**ry, no wet nor dry; seemed that floated presences unknown, that any **Thoughts** 'n **Thinks** theirs be known, to be heard 'n stood, in *Pains* 'n what would ... slowly they manifested, in Forms 'n Shapes; of **Souls 'n Spirits**: softly gliding softly biding their turn to explain their **L**ives 'n their strives ... then the **LIGHTS** dimmed 'n voices trimmed, without moans or groans, balanced with measured tones, to express their stories 'n their tales, when they lived in the Mounts 'n in the Vales !

" 'Twas a town versed, in the known 'n unknown: of **Arts** 'n **Crafts**„ of **Beauty** 'n Duty to one 'n other! Came a day, an **Evil** Sunday; when all were there 'n none a**S**tray: an **Evil** of a **Devil**, nor of Pity 'n nor of Piety ... Before we had lived in Unity 'n **Peace** 'n **Harmony** 'n Liaison ... but, but, but, this Intervention, so but so **Devilish**, like a Softy Soft Poison, infiltrated Discord 'n Dis-Union 'n Dis-Satisfaction ... 'tween Ourselves 'n 'tween Our Nears 'n 'tween Our Neighbours ... by so Simple such Means of *Jealousy*, of Selfishness, of Hate 'n of Pretension ... Everyone thinking that they were better than Others; 'n deserved better than others ... not to be mentioned that, since centuries, Such has been the Cause of the Fall of any Risen Nation, Empire 'n Civilisation ... "*Emperors* bygone, *Courtiers* bygone, *Flatterers* bygone, *Traitors* bygone, *All* bygone?

... **The Perfect Transition of *the Mighty to the Nighty*** ... (Original Story, was E. A. Poe)

Hut on the Hill 14/01/2017 Strange 'n Cynic

'Twas a strange combination, when I thought about 'The Hut on The Hill'! Ruminating it from afar„ it showed me the **Past** Visions **of Life**; the forgotten past lying in these dormant regions of my unconscious, that had none practical reality now ... they had been„ refreshing the real had-been, in the **L**ife afore? And when I visited it, accompanied by my **Love**, it lead me into a strange Visionary **World**, where strange beings from elsewhere took over, to learn to me a **L**ife estranged„ full of swells 'n **Waves** of imagined had-beens !!!

Happened again a **third** Time ... 'Twas this **T**ime a mitigated day, nor cold nor **W**arm, nor slow nor sped, neither lazy neither hazy ... Grass was **greyed**„ 'n Autumn delayed; door was open, no need to knock„ knock 'n knock ? Inside, a muffled laughter ... meeting **Lost Souls** roaming 'n flittering about, some in air or in stand by; holding **b**ellies: supressed laughter unuttered ... Welcoming us, **b**urst out loud; without sound, said: 'Just saw a funny thing, makes us **not** laugh; hi-hi' ? **Strange 'n Cynic** ??? 'N the story so revealed ...

" **V** just saw a couple of couples„ mad they were, but mad not all; **L**iving 'n thinking, Stories of Wonderland! Every woman was named **A**lice, but none had **M**alice, hi-hi! The **cat** on the Tree 'n the **oyster** in the **Sea**„ 'n a **walrus** biding-by his **T**ime; the Queen a dummy, who 'cut off' **h**eads but none fell down, seemed afraid for her own **C**rown! The Jester was a Valet 'n the Knight, not so Bright; 'n the whole Court lived on in a Hole„ a whole hole in a dreary **Earth**, that we call a **World**, hi-hi! Ô good-day, we've **N**o**thing** more to say, hi-hi! "

Funny story, without no beginning, no mid, no end: as **L**ife? Days after, thinking of the **H**ut, **M**emories came back, of when was I a young student! A Sunny day, I got a call ... **Tariq**, we're going to Spain! Surprise ... **W**hen **W**hy **W**hat, my **Mind** boggled? Three weeks from my eXams, I blabbered? **1** week study, **1** week Spain, **1** week revise; you've never failed. Full-Stop! By what Money ? We don't need money; **V** hitch-hike! What's that? **U** thumb your way down the street & **S**ome**body** gives **U** a lift to Spain to back; 'elementary, my dear Watson'! But why lil me? 'Cause **Ma**'ll never accept other (***this lady was a*** *Wild Forest Fire*!) Went so I, to see Historical Spain! " He put in his thumb & pulled out a plum & said what a good boy am I. "

Wild Forest Fire = Salima (62 yrs friendship) daughter of a dear Master ... **Faiz** Ahmed **Faiz**!

Enough post-cards are around, to see what happens there; my first hitch-hiking **experience** well ended„ saw most, cost least: then passed my eXams, **as easy as "two fingers in the nose"** (French saying). So a few months went as a **Charm** ... *then struck Destiny*! 'Twas 6th. September, 1965; a good morning, without warning, India attacked **Pakistan** and on all TVs we saw their armies marching thru the streets of **Lahore**, my home-town : 'twas **False** & later I learned that in All **World** Cities, Tokyo to N-York, was propagated this pre-planned complot (orchestrated a week before„ ('**Mensonge Mondial**') ... ***Internationalism's no Reality***.

So listened I to radio news for 30 seconds, every half of an hour; but my Office Manager asked me to stop it, what **Naturally** I refused: so was reported 'n convoked afore a C.A. Disciplinary Committee, where '*a hoard of* ***golden daffy-dils***' awaited me, of serious vacant **e**yes, **I's** all BritiX ... to their big surprise, I held that BritiX Law was based on '***commercial usage***', thus 'if my Office Manager, in Office, listened to a **Cricket Commentary** all day, I had same right, on important issues, to do same' ... so without a show of scratching **h**eads, these Oldered BritiX, scratched their **h**eads; for a BritiX, **Manager was a Manager** ... & this tradition had to be maintained, what be Cost to **Demon-Crazy** ??? But: **How-do-U-do**? **How**??? *Plz await the suite ...*

Hut on the Hill 15/01/**2017** **Soft 'n Sober**

the suite ... Re-convoked a few days later for verdict, saving both **f**aces of both arguments; 'twas a special case ... just render apologies 'n no action tc-ok ... seeing such **just** justice, I conceded; 'n all's well that ends well! But made I a request; *a concession, not a right* : to be granted, as rights facility ... of **6** months study leave, as my last eXams was **2** years after ! This also, mutually was accepted; and on the 13th. November, 1965, I flew off back home; a *hitch-hiking flight*! For now I me, a trained 'n experienced oldner was; hi-hi ...

Clad in light clads, behind White **C**liffs of Dover, freezing **Sea** re**M**inding, Winter settling in! **4** days in .Paris., friends **W**armly attired me: then the route to Strasbourg found me on the AutoBahn for Münich ... a car stopped; a hefty big 'n strong man descended; in a sweep he swung my ruck-sack into the dicky; inviting me in! Surprised was I? **NO Left-Leg** had? Surprise mine greater was? His driving partner, **No Right-Leg** had neither ... happily they drove, in care 'n in speed, perfect pairing as each completing other! Bid me they G'bye in Münich, where tc-ok me an Italian couple, to Italian border across Austria, **completely** snowed in ... 'twas unseen, for I had no **Visum-Italianum**„ but this couple refused to quit 'n waited: till the customs favoured me a special; 'n **S**milingly granted me an eXtraordinary permission 'Close **e**yes, no stamp' hi-hi ... Thus onto Bari, by car cart, or truck; where I tc-ok a boat onto Athens ... 'n all thanks to **friends unknown**.

The **fourth** **T**ime! 'The **H**ut on The **H**ill': 'twas another strange story. Me 'n my **Love** were now used to the unusual events; 'n this once, all was Calm 'n Quiet, **Soft 'n Sober**; the grass was green 'n the herb greener ... Inside there was no **Soul**, no **S**hadow, no scamper, no scurry, **but** **SHADES** bowing down in deep **Reflection**„ in so deep a meditation, that they noticed us not or hardly not„ as we entered, **h**ead shed!

Respecting this hush atmosphere, we susurrated to each other, what was 'n what was not; but one of the **spectres** finished 'n greeted us with soft **S**miles; saying, " If **Universe** wasn't„ know you what'ld pass in the **cosmos** ? We'll be there 'n not there ... 'twas what our meditation was about? " **Mein Gott**, that's a difficult theorem; we don't know, but do you? " We are on the way 'n find we'll out„ for that, we've never lacked! "

Then after a **T**ime, they came back with *Sparkling* **e**yes; " Supposing the **Universe** is **Not**„ then all's **Naught**! No Strife, no Struggle, nor **Nor**, nor **Not**, not What, nor Ought? Then what remains„ but Sought! **Seeking so's Believing**„ as without Believing, **N**othing, or **or**, or Anything exists Not! ***Yo***, ***Yond***, 'n ***BeYond***„ Levels, All Three„ here, there 'n here-after, in common terms„ we are, if We are Conscious„ that We are; otherwise are we Naught? You can ***Add*** them Not, you must ***Multiply*** them; so when there exists a Multiple of ***Knots***, ***Naughts***, or ***Nots*** ... exists already **So**mething„ a Consciousness of **So**mething; 'n **S**omething must **BE**: such's the Eternal **Natural** Law! Then if, **Something must** exist„ **Something has to** exist„ as **Obligation**! "

Our **h**eads buzzed, but we listened, attentive that there was **S**omething there! " Consequently, consent that a Negative is Negative, but Multitudes of Negatives is Positive„ thus only of **N**othing's born a **S**omething„ so in the Beginning there might have been No **Light**„ but **Lightly** came it 'n became Visible„ ***so 'twas always***„ it only tc-ok a Catalytic, to de-clench it ... If **Universe** was not, **Chaos** was„ in which **God** needed company, so's Created the **cosmos**„ on **Light** Forms 'n Other Forms„ namely **Us** En**Lightened**, to hold Company **???** "

Hut on the Hill 16/01/**2017** **Sound 'n Stable**

Thus 'twas, thus we talked, thus off 'n on, to each other. Thus separated we„ off 'n on; so learned always they me; a **So**mething anew: very learned, Phantoms or so they seemed! Or really, were they my old 'n respected masters, who taught me all 'n still were teaching me; whenever felt they, that 'twas needed! Who'll ever know? Never Perhaps! But counted I, always on them, 'n ever'll ... **O, V-Much Thanks Masters**!

Unimaginable, my mother's delight, enchanted when returned I to her; **8** delicious months passed. So short a few last months that I saw her in gɑɒd health„ in bliss 'n **Happiness**. Time passed positively; published few articles on complex subjects in so many a News-Papers (some reproduced in Vol-II; Bɑɒk-2 **p**-12-**095**-); acting in theatre, a **2** month loud applauded comic role in 'The Rope' of **A. Christi** ... 'n lots other things; **then bade a gɑɒd-bye to all**: to be back again ... In **1969** Mom fell to a coma lasting years **3**„ Ending 1972!

But my masters lack me. So afore close, I rendered them a last 'n **fifth** visit! Went I, me 'n my Love to knock on the dɑɒr ... surprisingly, it was already open; and inside, was all **Happiness**: masks off, I recognised many of my masters ... he taught me so, 'n he taught me so, 'n she taught me so ... they embarrassed me full, 'n offered me all they had; knowledge, gɑɒdies, joys, buts 'n nots! They opened the conversation, " Son you have been a gɑɒd learner, studious 'n **Reflective**, what gives us a lot of **Pleasure**; so today we have a last 'n best lesson for you ... **Do you know who you are** ? hi-hi! That's the only thing you have to learn in life ... **Know yourself 'n all Veils will Lifted be**; all **F**alse-hɑɒds Revealed! Want to try??? "

"**Humans 'r own worst enemy**; 'lil by 'lil, strata by strata, peel off all, denude yourself to **Completeness** be, afore a mirror; **none** more revealed: become **Soul 'n Spirit**, like us! Why to strip off all? Live: **Soul 'n Spirit**? Hiding yourself from yourself„ is Un-**Truth**; 'n **Un-Truth's Poison to Purity 'n Piety** ... **Worlds** of Visions 'n Illusions: **D**esires 'n Wishes; pasting Outer Layer of **F**alse-hɑɒd on yourself; to become an open bɑɒk to all, eXcept to yourself: so Ephemere becomes your Abode 'n your Domain: final be„ **Buried be your Truth**!"

Then they concluded ... "**Son**, you remain here, while we remain there 'n everywhere; you don't have to call us: we'll know when to come in your need. Then one day you'll join us 'n do the same as we do ... lead **Humanity** to gɑɒd, to **Truth**, to **Eternity**„ to become a part of **Eternity**: the only **Truth** that exists ... as **Sound 'n Stable** ! "

Years ago, the Hut on the Hill, was probably another Vision, of child-hɑɒd and purity; then **D**estiny changed a bit„ so, **the moving finger wrote 'n having writ moved on** ... nor all thy piety or nor all thy wit, will change a single line; or half a word of it ... (**Omar Khayyam**, who was a poët only in his free Time ... an enormous scientific, inventing a correct ***Solar Calendar, with 29th. February*** ... what later on was a bit 'stolen' by the **Vaticano**, to establish the Gregorian Calendar) ... [Consider : **August**us = Cæsor : **Sept**ember, sept = 7: **Oct**ober, octagon = 8: **Nov**ember, nove = 9: **Dec**ember, decimal = 10] ... Question ? How did appear the ***eXtra 2 months***??? Around the 15th Century, to re-establish the solar correction, the calendar was **ceased** about July, which **re-started** as September ... 'n hi-hi ... the Sun **was Corrected**„ hi-hi! ***Vive le Roy***!

I didn't write all this, to **Whine** 'n **Cry**„ I wrote, as the lady I **Love** asked me, "But I know **Nothing** of you?" So I said, "We'll **see**, we'll **see**, I promise we'll **see**." So I tɑɒk her out to **Sea**, what had been the **InComplete** of my **L**ife; for she„ being there, all other was **Complete**! **YOU but fell down to it as accessory**??? hi-hi. **End**.

Images (Public Domain) ... https://pixabay.com/ ... https://www.pexels.com/ ... https://unsplash.com/ ... https://www.publicdomainpictures.net/en/

Ser. #	Page	Description
1.	Title	https://www.gettyimages.fr/detail/photo/hot-tea-or-coffee-in-a-red-mug-cookies-book-and-image-libre-de-droits/1215917792?adppopup=true ... gettyimages-1215917792-612x612.jpg ... https://www.gettyimages.fr/detail/photo/fireplace-with-fire-burning-image-libre-de-droits/75406522?adppopup=true ... gettyimages-75406522-612x612.jpg ...
2.	3	ROSY ... **https://www.pexels.com/fr-fr/photo/soleil-couchant-amour-gens-femme-7137432/**
3.	3	**English** ... Beowulf ... http://www.pgdp.net ... Project Gutenberg ... 29 by Samuel Taylor Coleridge
4.	6/7	Roma ... **Vaticano** ... **Italiano** ... pexels-photo-6251682.jpeg ... https://www.pexels.com/photo/majestic-dome-ceiling-with-fresco-paintings-in-catholic-cathedral-6251682/
5.	6/7	Italia ... pexels-photo-970519.jpeg ... https://www.pexels.com/photo/bridge-of-sighs-venice-italy-970519/
6.	6/7	**Pakistan** ... **Lahore** ... **Punjab** ... **Islamabad** ... https://www.google.fr/search?q=lahore+historical+city&tbm=isch&tbo=u&source=univ&sa=X&ved=0ahUKEwi9gO610bjXAhXMyKQKHc_iAIkQsAQIOA
7.	6/7	**National.Chart.of.Accounts.fr** ... **My Own Written Chart of A/Cs ... on My Own Writ Site** http://www.noor-us-samaawat.com/documents/thQ-ChartNc.pdf
8.	6/7	**Unicode**.org Consortium ... **International Consortium ... All Computer Language Codes**
9.	6/7	NADRA Nat. IDs ... **Pakistan National Site for ID Cards ... Open to ALL Citizens of the World**
10.	6/7	**Microsoft** ... **Major International Site, for Computer Softwares ... Open to ALL World Citizens**
Most Pages		General Reference ... https://www.pexels.com/search/balochistan%20Pakistan/ ... https://www.pexels.com/search/ ...
11.	**-10-**	1. Qalat: **Baluchistan** **A Tale from Life** (9 years – 1950 Aug.) My First Story ... ... pexels-photo-415969.jpeg ... pexels-photo-815880.jpeg pexels-photo-5303058.jpeg ... ... pexels-photo-6182219.jpeg ... pexels-photo-5417955.jpeg ... pexels-photo-6018532.jpeg ...
12.	**-24-**	5. **Lahore**: **Punjab** **Adolescence** (13 years – 1954 Apr.) ... https://www.pexels.com/search/ ... pexels-photo-4610272.jpeg ... pexels-photo-2383832.jpeg ... ... pexels-photo-2240891.jpeg ... pexels-photo-2734406.jpeg ... ... pexels-photo-127753.jpeg : Lake Siaf ul Malook ... Siaf ul malook-05.jpg (Myself: Own Foto)
13.	**-40-**	7. **Lahore**: **Punjab** **A Study in Sounds** **Heard Not Seen** (15 years – 1956 Mar.) ... https://www.pexels.com/search/... pexels-photo-744667.jpeg ... pexels-photo-4035587.jpeg ... ... pexels-photo-4004375.jpeg ... pexels-photo-4298692.jpeg ... pexels-photo-5417957.jpeg ... ... pexels-photo-4043643.jpeg ... pexels-photo-3995673.jpeg ... pexels-photo-5721094.jpeg ...
14.	**-40-**	7. **Lahore**: **Punjab** **A Study in Sounds** **Heard Not Seen** (15 years – 1956 Mar.) ... https://www.pexels.com/search/... pexels-photo-3110502.jpeg ... pexels-photo-3726313.jpeg ... ... pexels-photo-210876.jpeg ... pexels-photo-1114690.jpeg ... pexels-photo-672636.jpeg ... ... pexels-photo-327509.jpeg ... pexels-photo-1719233.jpeg ... pexels-photo-342002.jpeg ...
15.	**-46-**	8. **Karachi**: **Sindh** **T'wink'ing Lights** (15 years – 1956 Aug.) ... https://www.pexels.com/search/balochistan%20Pakistan/ ... www.karachi.com/v/history/ ... ... https://www.pexels.com/photo/silhouette-photo-of-a-man-walking-on-seashore-during-sunset-3761178/ ... Sun ... https://www.pexels.com/search/Poetry/ ... https://www.pexels.com/photo/art-artistic-blank-page-book-371954/ ...
16.	**-51-** **-63-**	9. **Lahore**: **Punjab** Images : **A Rhythm of a Mind** (15 years – 1956 Dec.) ... https://pixabay.com/images/search/brain%20waves/ ... quantum-physics-4550602__340.jpg ... https://pixabay.com/vectors/brain-mental-health-think-5398414/ ... Penelope! ... pexels-photo-1118873.jpeg ... https://www.pexels.com/photo/quote-on-signboard-on-shabby-wall-near-bright-green-leaves-4371730/ ... https://pixabay.com/ ... pexels-photo-962312.jpeg ... pexels-photo-1020478.jpeg ... pexels-photo-1270184.jpeg ... 10. **Lahore** **Punjab** **ART for SENSE** (How to Write?) (**1957** - 15 years Jan.) ... https://pixabay.com/photos/taj-mahal-sunset-taj-mahal-india-4808227/ ... taj-mahal-sunset-4808227_960_720.jpg ... https://pixabay.com/ ... pexels-photo-1038935.jpeg (Infinity Road) ... pexels-photo-1210273.jpeg (Heart Breaks) ...
17.	**-74-**	12. **Hut on the Hill** 2007 (55 years Jan.) **Fifty years had passed** 4/10 https://www.pexels.com/search/ ... crete-78954_960_720.jpg ... lion-3676984_960_720.jpg ... ... sculpture-378280_960_720.jpg ... https://www.pixabay.com/photos/sculpture-art-aristotle-statue-3399968/ ...
18.	**-75-**	12. **Hut on the Hill** 2007 (55 years Jan.) **Fifty years had passed** 5/10 ... https://unsplash.com/photos/P_Ne56WEe5s photo-1554058922-d51b58b707f5.jpg (Mosque) ...

Further Reference and Consultation in details ... See ... **History**: https://www.pexels.com/search/balochistan%20Pakistan/

Healing with verse … Book of My Niece … Zahra

Homage to my Dear Niece : Daughter of Kausar Hameed (Kochi-ji) … A **True Image of my Mother**

Zahra Hameed debuts an Anthology of Poetry … Intimate Thoughts on Mental Health, Love & Relationships

Mental Health, no more is a Taboo: What in Past was Troublesome, is simply looked on now as a Brave 'n Courageous, that one Talks over it!

Burning Champa

Deciduous tree is an Apocynaceae: of Cultural Belief in most of Orient.

In a Similar Vein, Several of the DewaneZahra's Poëms in her Anthology allude to the Trepiditions and Joys of a Relationship 'tween a Man 'n a Woman. Zahra, it is possible, may even talk about herself … but the Emotions are Universal!

What does a Man do …

To make a Woman feel Loved?

A Man Notices Tiniest Things,

Like Un-fallen Tear in my Eye!

https://unsplash.com/s/photos/plumeria-rubra

Plumeria Rubra … photo-1619516794122-c189bb741a5f.jpg … photo-1619516947016-06223e8d61c8.jpg … photo-1599351334993-b7a1c6cd774f.jpg

Urdu Translation of some Sufiana Verses … (2021)

Zahra's Quatrain : **to whisper stories**

کہانیوں کی سنسناہٹ گزن ذھزن کی سرسراہٹ
پرچھائیوں کی حرکت دریچہ مینہ ٹپک ٹپک میں
آتش جلن کی دھک دھک پھر تمہارے اندر میں
گمشدہ گمشدہ تھکن تھک بند تمرے مندر میں !

07:37

To Whisper Stories
Of What We are going to do
Our Silouhettes move in Rainy Windows
So Burn I Slow 'n Fast … so, so Lost … Inside of You.

… Now Rendered to an Expanding Rhymed Quatrain …

My Brother at the Great Wall of China … (2008)

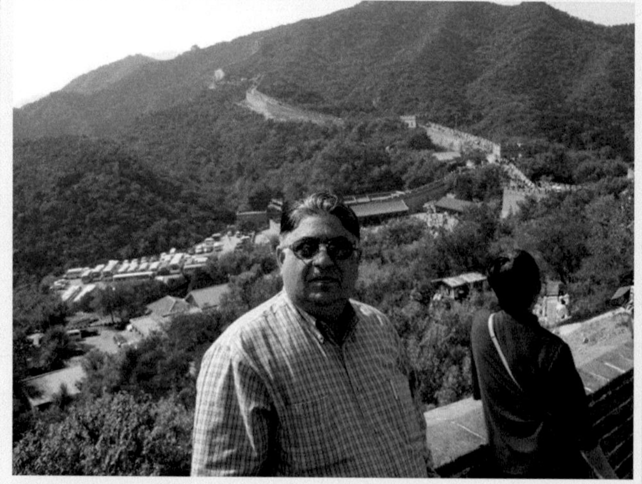

100. Troyes **Family Tree ... Hameed Sons ...** (**8 Generations Lahore**) Reality-8- (2019) -99--293-

G-G-**G**-G-**G**-Grand	7	Hafiz Allah Baksh	Qura'an	Memorised
G-**G**-G-**G**-Grand	6	Hafiz Hidayat Baksh	Qura'an	Memorised
G-G-**G**-Grand	5	Hafiz Qadir Baksh	Qura'an	Memorised
G-**G**-Grand	4	Hakeem Kareem Baksh	Hakeem	Medicine
Great-Grand	3	Hakeem Shams Deen	Hakeem	Medicine
Grand-Father	2	Mian Siraj Deen	(Supdt. Of a Directorate)	
Father	1	Khan Sahib Mian Abdul Hameed (**BA LLB**)	(LMSF) Dr. Begum Meraj Hameed **Suharwardi**	
Tariq (MA Eng. : ACA, Lon. : IT, Fr)		**Kausar** Hameed (MBA)	**Tahir**a Hameed (MSc)	

(**Hand written by Nazir Ahmed Jia'baji**) ... DG Lahore Municipal Corporation

Daughter Shaheena Married Shahnawaz Zaidi (Chairman Fine Arts : Lahore University)

Nazir A.J. was married to Mumtaz Apa ... Daughter of **M**aulvi **M**ohammad **A**zeem (My Ustad)

In the Musafir Qabaristan (Garhi Shahoo) we have many graves ... of the **two** parts of our Family

1. **Father** ... Syed Abdul Hameed : Mian Abdul Hameed : Mumtaz Apa : Begum Meraj Hameed
2. **Mother** ... About 20 of the Suharwardi (Khwaja) Family, including 5 of our maternal Uncles

---

The name of our Nana (Maternal Grand-Father) was Ghulam Mohammad ... Nani (Maternal Grand-Mother) was Ayesha Bibi or Begum ... per the Medical Degree of Khala Jan, found by younger son.

She passed in the year 1934 and Parveen Apa was born in 1931 ---all verified---

Sisters ... Sardar : Mumtaz (Married **S**. **A**. **H**ameed) : Meraj : Saeeda (2nd of **S.A.H.**)

Sardar Married **M**aulvi **M**ohammad **A**zeem (My Ustad) ... Had Naseem; Parveen; Naeem.

Maulvi **M**ohammad **A**zeem (My Ustad) ... Married 4 Times (Never 2 together) Sardar was 4th.

Syed Abdul Hameed ... Married twice ... Mumtaz died (Sutan; Kishwar) ... then Saeeda (Nasreen)

Our Maternal Grand Father, Ghulam Mohamad, was the first Muslim Magistrate in Kashmir ... Poisoned

Ayesha Bibi or Begum was left a Widow, with 4 girls ... their only brother died at an early age.

Sardar & Meraj became Doctors : **L**udhiana **M**edical **S**chool for **F**emales ---of 1st. Batch---

The Brother of Nana, Sagheer **Suharwardi**, then looked after the entire Family.

Meraj became the Superintendent of Bostel Jail Lahore ... for Political Grand Dames.

She knew all Grand Ladies of India thus ... to the extent of playing cards with Indra Ghandi.

Indra, as Prime Minister, invited her to India on an Official Visit: being now a Widow, she could not go.

1960

elle

avait

17

ans

Puis … Tout Frais du Pakistan :

je me suis trouvé à Londres

et j'ai posé une demande

pour Concours de

l'Harmonica à

Straßbourg

en 1963

…

Tariq Hameed … Personal History

… Nicole-Jordy.wpl : Championne de Monde d'Harmonica …

… 1965 : Delft Hollande : **Accordion Times-00- -88-** …

Dedicated to Nicole … of forty-eight years of friendship … we always disputed with each other„ but I we felt and insisted **that** we knew but each other since a half of a century … where she always corrected me; 'minus something' … **that** 'minus something' has materialised now to 'minus two', for the two of us„ since 2010: 'n not 2„ **she being the 'minus'**, unfortunately.

And I always hoped and promised her, **that** we will laugh full **that** day, when the half became the full: but it didn't, so my promise was broke„ for none fault of mine's or hers … only let's say, I was well punished; for I broke her heart: **and to this day, I suffer**; for how could an empty promise come to be fulfilled: **things broken have never an end, 'Cause Ends 'Tis-selves can't Never Mend 'Tis-self!** Thus is the Eternal Law of Nature …
How? Explain me **that**! Nothing now can ever change, as all Ends? **Well or Well Not**„ 'n **that is that** …

Ada Massaro ... Pittrice Italiana ... Nata a Lecce 1949, poì a Roma ... e *Svizzera*, Neunburg ... **Personal History**

Ada e Tariq : a la sua Casa, Roma, 2010 ...

Denise : sua figlia e mia Tina, Roma ... 1985

Painting in my Personal Possession

My German Grand-Mother ... (Germany/Deutschland *Offenburg*) ... Meine Deutsche GrossMutter

... Tariq Hameed and Renate Geppert ... Meine Deutsche GrossMutter ... in der Nähe von Schwartzwald ...

Tariq Hameed ... Personality Signature Analysis (Deutschland Hannover 1993)

1. *Upper & Lower* ***Loops***

1.1. **Intelligence**: Even height & depth shows a person acting intuitively, with no compelling reason to think analytically, preferring to rely on internal feelings and unexplained intuitions ... as "raison d'être" of Active 'n Acting Reason.

1.2. **Emotions**: Thus following an accordance with the intimate **Thoughts**, making no great demands on life; content with the own self and all that's around.

2. *Spacing Characteristics*

2.1. **Will-Power**: Density shows eagerness to try all out in full innocence; resolutely with enthusiasm, trying to complete tasks even less pleasant.

2.2. **Character**: Optimistic, enjoying daily aspects of life; the cheerful and vivacious manner enabling to solve even most difficult problems in an original way.

3. *Breadth & Style Formations*

3.1. **Communication**: Ability, of a very approachable attitude; talkative without any indiscretion & able to keep all told secrets, securely in confidence.

3.2. **Vitality**: Challenges attacked without hesitation: exerting strength & mastering problems by a fresh & lively method, as energy lasts; but making last surely.

Scope Analysis (Left Palm Image)

4. *Internal & Personal Matters*

4.1. **Character**: U may work far from home, experiencing many changes in life & working quite late old; sharp & capable, good planner who works out simple solutions to complicated problems. This talent which few people possess, when properly cultivated, enables U to make new & effective discoveries.

4.2. **Love & Marriage**: Quarrels can arise timely during courtship, due to your strong will & habits. Quite a few disappointments in love affairs will come, taking a lot of time for wound healing. This as from your young age,, may make U miss your chance to marry; but U may well succeed **Late to Mate**.

5. *External & Worldly Matters*

5.1. **Career & Money**: Your family background made U mature early, enjoying a comfortable life young. U dilly-dally & slack of old, risking so to squander early fortune; don't procrastinate, work harder to have NOT regrets older. Eager to succeed, your anxiety can lead U to fail, that may not even ends meet; so be patient & slow down: to GAIN by acting prematurely NOT.

5.2. **Health**: Quite healthy & energetic, U care for yourself. Be not over confident, as minor ailments ignored, can do harm: if giddy, check blood pressure.

6. *General Advice*

6.1. **To Know What & How to do is Good** : But ***When to do is better***. Act timely; **Wait**?

6.2. **Being Capable U reason out How to Act** : *Timing is important:* the jealous may feel well, that probably, may U like it or not ...
your high performance, is designed to vaunt to belittle others.

Character Analysis (of 2012) ... Tolerance to Routine

- **Style**: Supple and Accepting ... In a global manner, you live a life, organised and well structured: not tending to bow to Newness and Variety, at any price; only Leaning to Necessity, **if Reason Be**! You are at Ease, in your mundane habits and manners ...
your Past 'n your Present in One Self ... in special, for your Future 'n a Better-Half Self!
- Fundamentally, you need to dedicate yourself to a person, who professes Righteous and Exclusive Love Terms, mutually. However, your tolerance to feeble phantasies ...
shows a goodness 'n a greatness of your Heart 'n your Soul: a sole goal role!
- You disdain the Concept of Oscillating Engagements, or of Total Liberty; which goes against your Concept of the Purity of Sentiments ...
You desire sharing the "**Good 'n Bad**" moments, **in common 'n in calm**!
- Even if you like to maintain a permanent liaison with your natal family, but it precludes not, that you blab-out all to all 'n every: so you maintain a reasoned **balance** ...
balancing your **Self**: 'tween **your own 'n your else**!
- Your Elderly Style is "Democratic": so certain connivance and a true Effective Proximity, in all your Relationships; be it towards the Superiors or Inferiors. That, the limits be considered limits true, of structured rapports, 'tween Equals 'n Similar: constructing ...
a **harmonious 'n so stable a union**, as practical as possible!
- In your opinion, a balanced Education, as well for Elders, as well for Juniors, rigorous 'n effective, leaving Structural Betterment for both, is the Call of the Day ...
a simple **Call to Comfort, generating Traces of Stability and of Elegance**!
- Etymologically speaking, **Masks** are the Essentials of your Life ... the Notion of the **Mask**, dating from the Old Ages, from Three Gongs of Destiny of the Theatres of Antiquity; 'n of **Masks** of Argil, ably borne by the Actors of Yester-Days? "**Life is a tale, told by an Idiot**" ... of **Masks**,
Masks which **Hide 'n Masks** which **Reveal,** which of which **Truths 'n** which **Falsity of Life**!
- Your Personality is the **Hidden Story**,, be Revealed or Un-Revealed, to these **Strangers** called "**Men**". Thus, our Being is Touched by What is Open 'n What is Closed: these Variations of Comportment, our Real 'n True Inner-self,, times often which Cries; 'n times some which Laughs ... so ...

Soul-less or full; Suffers or Beatifies our Core 'n our Corpse ... what so Constitutes our Mental?

Tariq Hameed ... Kalai-ka-Thakhta ... The Wrist Key-Board for Urdu, Arabic, Farsi & Turkish ... MQZ (National Language of Pak)

NATIONAL LANGUAGES AUTHORITY PAKISTAN   مقتدرہ قومی زبان   اردو کمپیوٹر کلیدی تختہ : ورژن ۱۰۰۰

Committee Convenor TARIQ HAMEED

Esc | F1 F2 F3 F4 | F5 F6 F7 F8 | F9 F10 F11 F12

Tab ... Q W E R T Y U I O P [ ] \ ... OXOF

Caps Lock Shift II ... A S D F G H J K L ; ... ENTER

SHIFT ... Z X C V B N M < > ? ... SHIFT

Ctrl | Alt | SPACE | Alt Shift III | Ctrl

UR-Sy-B = Urdu Symbol Begin , E = End

Except: Alt Gr or Shift 2 This is Functional Now as Arabic + Farsi + Urdu

Original in Cabinet Div.

Since 1999 on a GLOBAL Level:

Urdu "Atomic" Keyboard (ARABIC SCRIPT) PAK.

It is now the PAKISTAN NATIONAL STANDARD

ا (Alif) is 13.07 % of Tot. Usage
So ... It is placed on Right Index
(Strongest & Fastest Key Operator)

Particularity:

1. 61% of language is on pure "HOME KEYS"
2. Attains speeds of 210 letters per minute
3. WRIST Based (Not Elbow: like AZERTY/QWERTY)
4. "Atoms" can create 2000+ new Alphabet Letters
   ex.: e, é, è, ê, ë ... ë = e + ¨ (2 Atoms)
   ex.: c, ć, č, ĉ, ç ... ç = c + ̧ (2 Atoms)

Includes ALL Search Engines
*Expl...
*Goog...
*Unmst

Advantage: MS Stole ... Theft made it GLOBAL
Universal European Alphabet 26 + ? Atoms
e.g.: o, ó, ò, ô, ö = o ´ ` ^ ¨ ... ø o/ etc.
So V can have /Ainsi ... Universal Latin Keyboard

Stolen by my Accord

Normal Speed = 135 Lets!

TH Keyboard works at **210**

100 Million IDs in 6 mths

.1. Letter-Shape Grouped

.2. 61% Letters on Home

.3. Wrist + Finger NO Arm

.4. New Letters Creatable

.5. Easier for Youngsters

.6. Shift II Spurs 3rd. Let!

.7. To Universal Cultures!

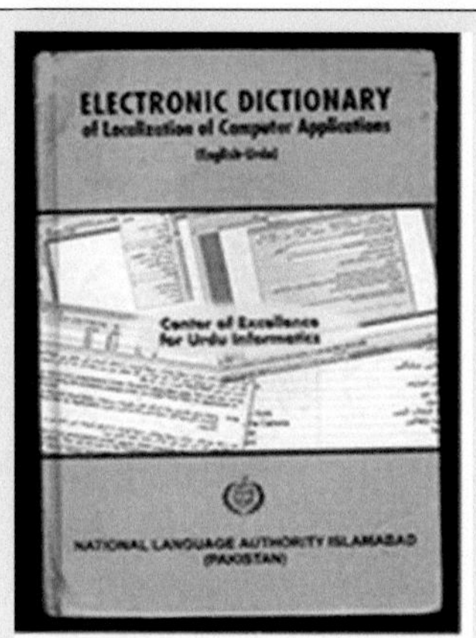

Urdu Tariq Computer
Microsoft Sponsored

This is the Story of my Life : in 3-D Colours ... as "Muqamaat"

Like a Qirat High-Lighted in 3-D Space ... by the "Vibrating Variations" of Voice

Tariq Hameed ... Kalai-ka-Thakhta ... The Wrist Key-Board for Urdu, Arabic, Farsi & Turkish ... MQZ (National Language of Pak)

Microsoft مقتدره قومی زبان، پاکستان

National Language Authority

Govt. of Pakistan, Cabinet Division

Microsoft Office and Windows XP

Microsoft Urdu Localization Project 2004-05 (1 Year)

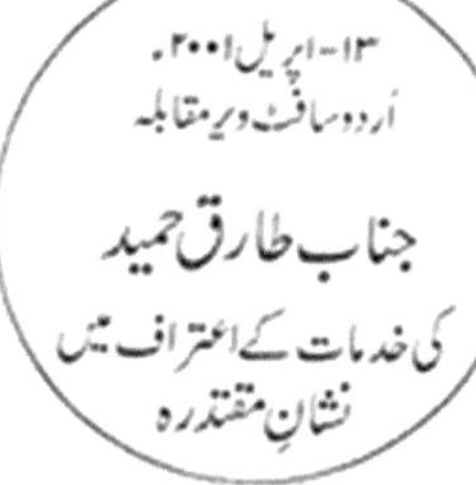

Memo of Participation

Certified that that Mr. Tariq Hameed

جناب طارق حمید

has been associated with the Project as

(Technical Validater) ٹیکنیکل ویلیڈیٹر

He performed his duties with full passions and hardworking. He has carried out his duties diligently qualifying the standards of Microsoft tasks and needs of Urdu assigned to him were found magnificent.

پروفیسر فتح محمد ملک
Prof. Fateh Muhammad Malik
Chairman

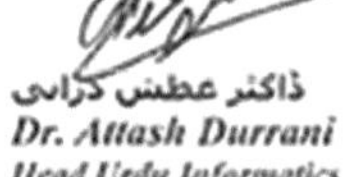

ڈاکٹر عطش درانی
Dr. Attash Durrani
Head Urdu Informatics

.1. Letter-Shape Grouped

.2. 61% Letters on Home

.3. Wrist + Finger NO Arm

.4. New Lets: New Scripts

.5. Military Codes Ability

.6. Line.1 30: 2. 61 3. 9%

.7. For Universal Usages!

طارق حمید

Urdu Seminar
06/06/1999

1st. Software Urdu Pak Competition Tariq Hameed Was the True Heart & Soul

NATIONAL LANGUAGE AUTHORITY PAKISTAN
FULL MEMBER OF UNICODE INC.

اُردو سافٹ ویئر کا اوّلین مقابلہ و نمائش

FIRST URDU SOFTWARE COMPETITION & EXHIBITION

Urdu Computer in 30 seconds: 1. Windows 2. Parameters 3. Date & Language 4. Add 5. Apply & 6. End

Atomic Alphabet: Letters, Dots, Accents (Top/Low) Atomised ... (UniCode '**Diacritics**') ... **7** Concat-Images.

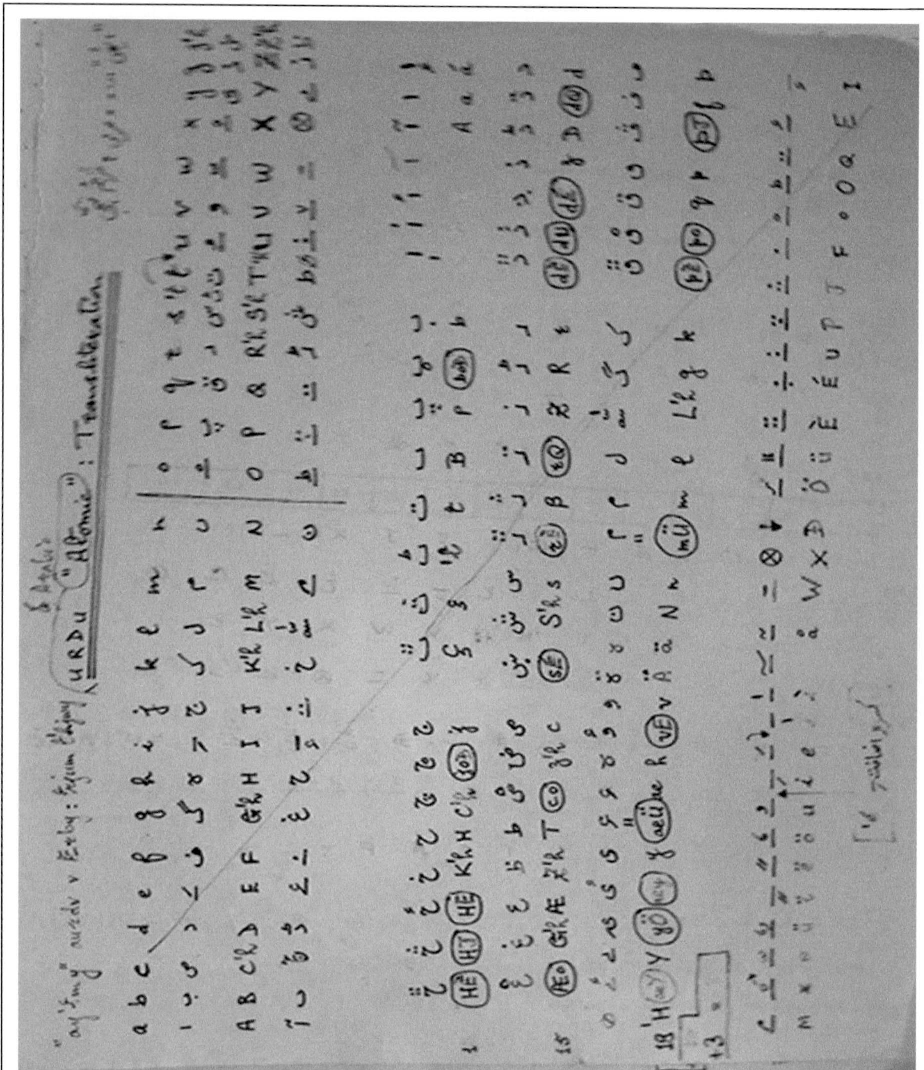

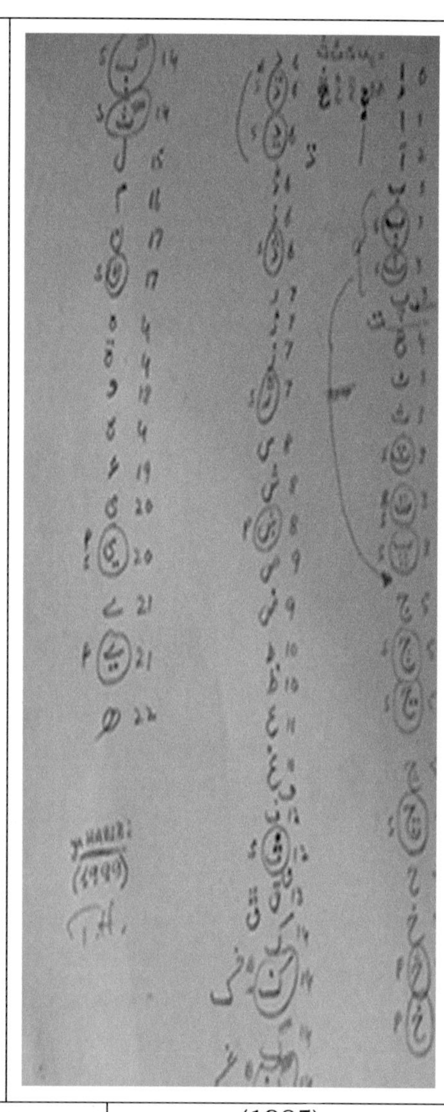

(2019)

European Atomic Alphabet ... 13*4=52 (a pack of cards)

a b c d e f g h i j k l m * n o p q r s t u v w x y z

A B C D E F G H I J K L M * N O P Q R S T U V W X Y Z

ä ç é è ê ë ï ö ü Ä Ç É È Ê Ë Ï Ö Ü (French)

à á á ã å æ ì í î ð ñ ò ó ô õ ø ß ù ú ú û ý ÿ þ

À Á Á Ã Å Æ Ì Í Î Ð Ñ Ò Ó Ô Õ Ø ß Ù Ú Ú Û Ý Ÿ Þ

^ ˇ ˈ ‒ ˊ ˋ ˘ ˚ ~ ˛ = etcetera

ˌ ‒ ˏ ˇ

Arabic

(1985)

Urdu Computer in 30 seconds: 1. Windows 2. Parameters 3. Date & Language 4. Add 5. Apply & 6. End

... Red ... Atomic Digit Letters ... Super-Imposed Diacritics ... Multiply Posed Image Elements ...

(Animation) http://www.noor-us-samaawat.com/#A1E5.1. (Slide Bar ... Next)

دوذ و دوزخ، دوذ و دوزخ؛ شرم تم کو ابھی نہیں آتی :

کعبہ کی سمت ہے کیا؟ یاں یا واں یا کاں ؟ بر نہیں آتی!

اور جب تھا قدم طارق کا، دہلیز باہر و اندر میں؛

تو شدّاد و غدّار کیا ؟ کیا عاقبت بھی دکھ نہیں آتی ؟

... "ابجد اردو بر قرآنی طرز" ... مکمّل ... {۲۰۱۸/۱۰/۲۹}

... یوں جیسے دستی کتابت ... ا ... ح ... د ... ر ... ر ... س ... ع ... مجّنہ علیحدہ ...

ا. . (ة).ب. . .خ. .ذ. .ر. .س. .ض. .ظ. .غ. . . . .ں. . . .و.ہ.ی.ئ.(ے). صلے

.1.

Under is Hell,
Under in Hell;
Ashamed are you Not:

.2.

Which Way Lies Prayer?
Here, There, Where?
Ashamed but you Not!

.3.

And When,
Puts Foot down Tariq,
In 'n Out Door-step unto:

.4.

Then Who Low is
or Traitor is?
Ashamed of Thy
Fate, are Thee Not?

(Animation) http://www.noor-us-samaawat.com/#A1E5.1. (Slide Bar ... Next)

ہم کو ہم کو، نہ آنا نہ جانا، یاں ہی اَست و بَست ؛

نزول تم کو ہونا نہیں یارو: کہ سب ہیں از خود میں مست !

اور جب تک رواں رواں رہے دنیا میں طارق ، یوں کستی میں؛

تو آتش و عطش کیا ہے ہوں ؟ بہا ناروں میں، دست بہ دست!

... "ابجد اردو بر قرآنی طرز" ... مکمّل ... {۲۰۱۸/۱۰/۳۱}

... یوں جیسے دستی کتابت ... ح ... ر ... کستی ... س ... مجّنہ علیحدہ ...

ا.ب.ت.(ة).ب.ج.ح.خ.د.ذ.ر.ز.س.ش.ص.ض.ط.ظ.ع.غ.ف.ق.ک.ل.م.ن.ں.و.ہ.ی.ئ.(ے). صلے

.1.

We 'n All Us We,
Nor Come Nor Go;
Here's Our Be Or Is;

.2.

Friends you are but
No-Where, Any-Where?
All in In-Self but Is!

.3.

And When,
Floats a World Tariq,
Sail Ships Sad Seas unto:

.4.

Then Fire 'n or
Thirst What is?
A Floating Flame,
Desolate in Desolate Is?

12. Roma : Italia : Italiano **Sonno Profondo** **Deep Sleep** -22--54--143- (1993)

tranquilla
profonda
perché
un sonno
cosa c’è
è un **Pensiero** della **Mente**
un stato di **Mente**
chi non **mente**
mai si **mente**
a se stesso
perché io
quando sogno
vedo la **Verità**
chi non esiste
in questo **Mondo**
e cosi preferisco
rimanere
solo un sonno
un sonno profondo
chi si sveglierà
quando ci serà
sola la **Verità**
la **Verità** **sola**
ma tutta la **Verità**
solo la **Verità**
Eterna e profonda
come può essere
un sogno
tranquillo
Warm
umano
e **Vero**
Vero sogno
della verità **Eterna**
nel sonno **profondo**

tranquil
profound
because
a sleep
what’s it
it’s **Minds’** **Thought**
a state of **Mind**
that **lies** not
lies never
to itself
because I
when I dream
I see **Truth**
that doesn’t exist
in this **World**
and so I prefer
to remain
only a sleep
a deep sleep
which will awake
when there’ll be
alone **Truth**
Truth **alone**
but all the **Truth**
and only but **Truth**
Eternal and profound
as can be
a dream
calm
Warm
human
’n **True**
a dream true
of **Truth** **Eternal**
in **deep** sleep

In Three WORDS; Ein WALZ'ER

Reflection-2-

40. Offenburg Deutsch (1994) … *thBk-E-05b*53-yrs*.pdf … -24--123-

	Hören Sie den walz; wie ♫♪u'sik. Klaps lass lass; klips lass lass. So so so; komm komm komm.	Hier gehen wir; Klaps auf eins. Wie Straus "Schön; Don'au Blau". Klaps zwei drei; Spitz auf vier.
1.	**Eins zwei drei; vier fünf sechs.**	**Eins zwei drei**; wollen wir tanzen.
2.	*Eins zwei drei*; und wollen walz wir.	*Eins zwei drei*; Ich liebe dich.
3.	Du liebst mich; *vier fünf sechs.*	In drei Worten; sagst mir was.
4.	Und war nicht; *vier fünf sechs.*	Wie geht's dir; meine süsse Liebe.
5.	Sag mir nicht; *weiß ich alles.*	*Eins zwei drei*; wir zwei alle.
6.	Brauchen wir nicht; eins oder drei.	Sind wir alle; wir zwei auch.
7.	Eins für zwei; zwei für einen.	*Eins zwei drei*; *vier fünf sechs.*
8.	Komm süsse Liebe; sieh mich an.	Sprecht gerade nicht; Blick Blick Blick.
9.	Ich habe dich; du liebst mich.	*Eins zwei drei*; wir wir wir.
10.	Du und ich; *vier fünf sechs.*	Lassen uns tanzen; ich und du.
11.	In meinen Armen; du für mich.	Ich für dich; und kein anderer.
12.	Aber sie draußen; kann dort bleiben.	Du bist mein; *vier fünf sechs.*
13.	*Eins zwei drei*; sagst mir alle.	Schlaf du gut; gut gut gut.
14.	Stellt deinen Kopf; auf meinem Arm.	Kuss kuss kuss; auf deiner **L**ippe.
15.	Ich liebe dich; *vier fünf sechs.*	Und mehr mehr; mehr als mehr.
16.	*Eins zwei drei*; wird nicht enden.	Weil wir zwei; jemals wird lieben.
17.	Bis zum Ende; als vielmehr:	Bis zu Allein; Wer uns sieht:
18.	Es nimmt uns; außer dem Ende.	Halten von Händen; süsse süsse Liebe.
19.	Eins ein ein; für mich ich.	Du für mich; ich für dich.
20.	Ohne Ende dann; *vier fünf sechs.*	Aber mehr mehr; mehr als mehr.
21.	*Eins zwei drei*; Gott und du.	Du und ich; in drei Wörtern.
22.	Du ich Gott; in darüber hinaus.	Und darüber hinaus; Gott du ich.
23.	Alle wir drei„ **G**ott du ich;	**G**ott **D**u ich: **G**ott **D**u **I**ch.
24.	*Eins zwei drei*; *eins zwei drei* …	… … … … … … … … …

Engagiert : *meiner Edlen Prinzessin Wiens* … ***Gertrud von Wien*** …

… gelesen werden kann … **in jeder Richtung** (alle 4) … … **gelesen umgekehrt, im romantischen Stil** …

tayles 'tween struts 'n frets ... 1 **THINKS 'n THOUGHTS**

Book 05a 1993 Volume Themes IV

...

tayles 'tween struts 'n frets ... 2 THINKS 'n THOUGHTS

Book 05b 1994 Volume Themes IV

...

tayles 'tween struts 'n frets ... 3 THINKS 'n THOUGHTS

Book 05c 1995 Volume Themes IV

Book 02 LIVRE 02 -3--92-

Book 04 LIVRE 04 1-32--121-

Book 06 LIVRE 06 -1--55--144-

CONTENTS **BOOK 3** French & English **Volume 1/2**

INDEX **THINKS 'n THOUGHTS 1974 ===> 1987** PENSER sur PENSÉES

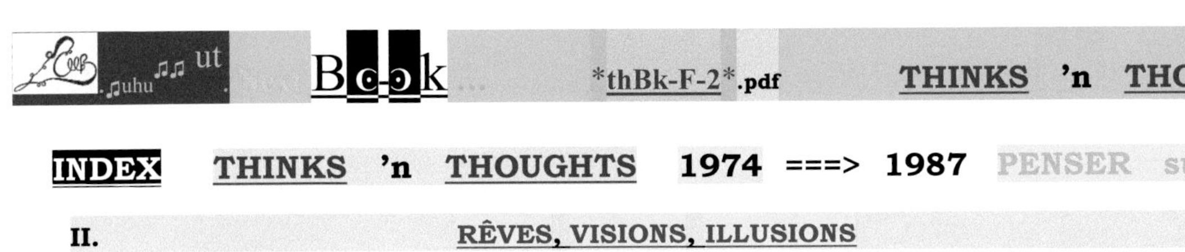

INDEX THINKS 'n THOUGHTS 1974 ===> 1987 PENSER sur PENSÉES

https://unsplash.com/ photo-1610208613897-03b8f139d2a6.jpg

photo-1486896427952-71586fb5976a.jpg

-1- -xiv-*I*014.

Prediction

Extra Bright

Full Moon

Occured ...

in December

22, 1999

photo-1606837753247-45e5f588d539.jpg

Full Moon 1901

https://unsplash.com/

THE OLD FARMER'S ALMANAC PREDICTS :

This year the full moon will occur on the Winter Solstice (December 22nd) called the first day of winter. Since the full moon on the winter Solstice will occur in conjunction with a lunar perigee (point in the moon's orbit that is closest to Earth) The moon will appear about 14% larger than it does at apogee (the point in its elliptical orbit that is farthest from the Earth) ... Since the Earth is also ... several million miles closer to the sun at this time of the year than in the summer, sunlight striking the moon is about 7% stronger making it brighter. Also, this will be the closest perigee of the Moon of the year since the moon's orbit is constantly deforming.

If weather's clear and there's snow cover by you,
it is believed that car headlights will be superfluous.

Full moon at Perigee & at Apogee … A Portuguese amateur astronomer António Cidadão, captured these images of the full Moon on two different dates using a black-and-white QuickCam on a 4-inch f/6.3 Schmidt-Cassegrain telescope. In the left-hand image the Moon was at perigee, i.e., closest to Earth. In the right-hand image it was at apogee, i.e., farthest from Earth. the differences in the Moon's size, are quite ... apparent

SKY & TELESCOPE RESPONSE: **Brightest Moon in 133 Years**?

Per Roger W. Sinnott, associate editor of Sky & Telescope magazine, the answer is an unequivocal: **No**!

It is true that there is a most unusual coincidence of events this year. As S&T contributing editor Fred Schaaf points out in the December 1999 issue of Sky & Telescope, "The Moon reaches its very closest point all year on the morning of December 22nd. That's only a few hours after the December solstice and a few hours before full Moon. Ocean tides will be exceptionally high and low that day." But to have these three events -- lunar perigee, solstice, and full Moon -- occur on nearly the same day is not especially rare. The situation was rather similar in …

December 1991 and December 1980, as the following dates and Universal Times show:

Event	Dec. 1999	Dec. 1991	Dec. 1980
Full Moon	22, 18h	21, 10h	21, 18h
Perigee	22, 11h	22, 9h	19, 5h
Solstice	22, 8h	22, 9h	21, 17h

What really rare is, is that in 1999 the three events take place in such a quick succession. On only two other occasions in modern history have the full Moon, lunar perigee, and December solstice coincided within a 24-hour interval, coming just 23 hours apart in 1991 (as indicated in the preceding table) and 20 hours apart back in 1866. The 10-hour spread on December 22, 1999, is unmatched at any time in the last century and a half.

So is it really true, as numerous faxes and e-mails to Sky & Telescope have claimed that, the Moon will be brighter this December 22nd, than at any time in the last 133 years ? We have researched the actual perigee distances of the Moon throughout the years 1800-2100, and here are some perigees of "record closeness" that also occurred at the time of full Moon:

Century	Date	Distance (km)	Date	Distance (km)
19 th.	1866 Dec. 21	357,289	1893 Dec. 23	356,396
20 th.	1912 Jan. 4	356,375	1930 Jan. 15	356,397
21 st.	1999 Dec. 22	356,654	2052 Dec. 6	356,421

It turns out, then, that the Moon comes closer to Earth in the years 1893, 1912, 1930, and 2052 than it does in either 1866 or 1999. The difference in brightness will be exceedingly slight. But if you want to get technical about it, the full Moon must have been a little brighter in 1893, 1912, and 1930 than in either 1866 or 1999, (based on the calculated distances).

The 1912 event is undoubtedly the real winner, because it happened on the very day the Earth was closest to the Sun that year. However, according to a calculation by a Belgian astronomer Jean Meeus, the full Moon on January 4, 1912, was only 0.24 magnitude (about 25 percent) brighter than an "average" full Moon.

In any case, these are issues only for the Astronomical Record Books. This month's full Moon won't look dramatically brighter than normal. Most people won't notice a thing, despite e-mail chain letters, implying that we'll see something amazing.

Our data is from the U.S. Naval Observatory's ICE computer program, Jean Meeus's Astronomical Algorithms, page 332; and the August 1981 issue of Sky & Telescope, **page 110.** **Question is … Can our OooolllooоO-e-aaaAMMMMAaaa Calculate so ???**

Nota : Date of Grand Prophets … J. Christ … Before C (in Minus -) … After C (in Plus +) … Christ Ô Christ Ô Christ ?

Hi Hi … Very Good Mathematicians SIR … Where's the YEAR ZERO 0000 ???? … False Gregorian Cal. by 1 yr … Hi Hi

1. This year the full moon will occur on the **Winter Solstice** (December 22nd) … named the **First day of Winter**

2. The full moon on the winter solstice will occur **in conjunction with a Lunar Perigee** … (point in the moon's orbit that is closest to Earth)

3. The **moon will appear about 14% larger** than it does at **Apogee** … (point in its elliptical orbit that is farthest from the Earth)

4. Since the Earth is ***also several million miles closer to the sun at this time of the year*** … than in summer, **sunlight striking the moon is about 7% stronger making it brighter**

5. Also, this will be the **closest perigee of the Moon of the year** … since the *moon's orbit is constantly deforming*

6. If the weather is clear and there is a snow cover where you live … *it is well believed that* … **car headlights will be superfluous**

Other Facts are … 22nd. December 1999 Full Moon … (Tariq Hameed) 

7. This full moon lay in the **Month of Ramadhan** (Islamic Year) … Astronomy proves … *that Ramadhan generally remains around the middle of year, at the Turn of Century*

8. Further, history proves that '*Ramdhan*' **seldom** divides itself over the Turn of a Century

9. However, this time 'twas a Miracle … the Turn of a Millennium … **never to happen again**

10. *Thus, we can Conclude that* … "Light Will Dawn Again on a Sleeping Civilisation"

11. *Strangely*, a couple of days later, i.e., the Night of 24-25 December (*'Xmas & Boxing Day*), there was a violent storm in Europe, with Winds flowing at over 170 km p/h, completely destroying the entire Electric System of ALL European Countries … … Only in France, more than 3 million Trees were Up-rooted … & In-spite of Free Govt. Gift, some are still lying around … Abandoned …

12. As a Result, the **wHole** of Europe and **mϾ-Ͽst** of America **passed in Darkness at 'Xmas**

13. *It can be Supposed* … that this **Play of Light & Darkness** … have *Hidden Surprises for us*

14. *Also to be remembered,* that Events Occurring on Turn of Centuries, have **long time life span**

… Examples are a Real Wonder … … to cite a few …

- **1495** AD … **Error** of Christophorus Columbus … ***Discovering America,*** instead of India
- **1565** AD … Siege of Malta : Followed by **Lépante** … ***Turks Lost*** *Sea Supremacy for ever*
- **1595** AD … Elisabeth I & **Shakespeare** … *Begins British Empire* : **English Domination**
- **1699** AD … **January 26** : **Treaty of Karlowitz** (Turkey & Venice, Poland, Austria) … ***Turks quit C-Europe***
- **1795** AD … The **French Revolution** … Base of the ***Modern Republics*** and ***Democracy***
- **1895** AD … The Planetary **Industrial Revolution** … *Colonialism* falls into a *Death Phase*
- **1995** AD … Starts an '**Age of Illumination**' … *Justice to Prevail* ... **IF** Humans want to Survive

'Twas my main Reason … *in Advance I Knew* … a Dominant Event of FUTURE.

The Rise of a LOST Civilisation … I SAW this **mΘ-Θn** … & I Knew What I had TO DO. **NooR us Samaa waT**

… Thus I Launched this Struggle to **Establish Urdu in Pakistan**, starting with Computer ID Cards …

… There was Dr. Chaudri (Patron) : TH (Brains) … Habibullah, Saeed Ahmed, Imran Qureshi (*& Action*) …

If Only 5 dedicated persons can change a Destiny, a Future … Let us **ALL** get together … **Wake UP Humanity**?

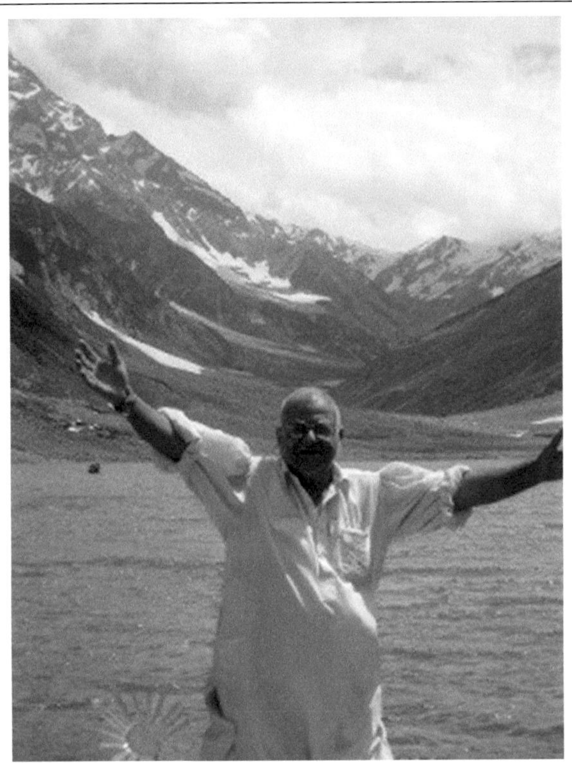

… Visible … be … …اللّٰہِ…ھَےْ…فَرْیَادِیْ…نَقشْ…
…Visible…soit… ……… …immer…ist…
…
…Traversée…des… nges…… ngels …here…Toe-Tip…

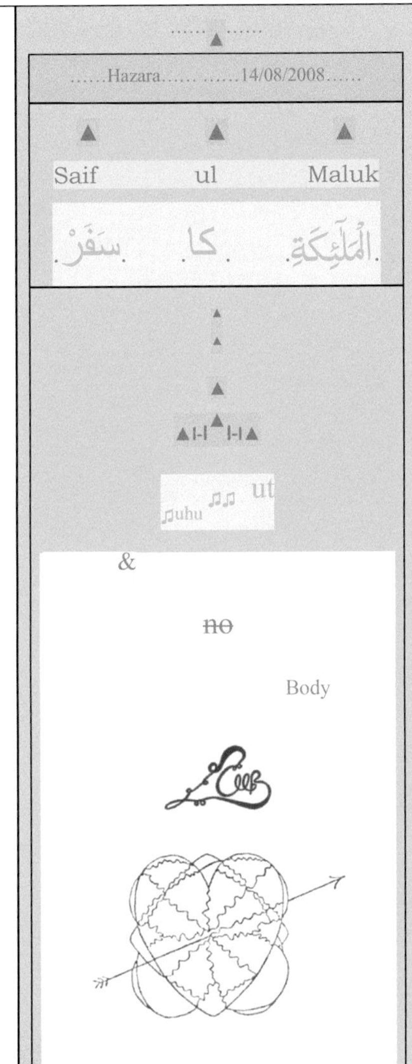
……Hazara…… ……14/08/2008……
Saif ul Maluk
.اَلْمَلَآئِکَۃِ. .کا. .سَفَرْ.
uhu ut
&
no
Body

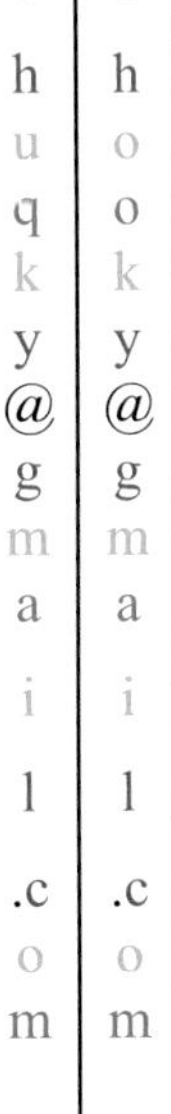
thuqkyy@gmail.com
thookyy@gmail.com

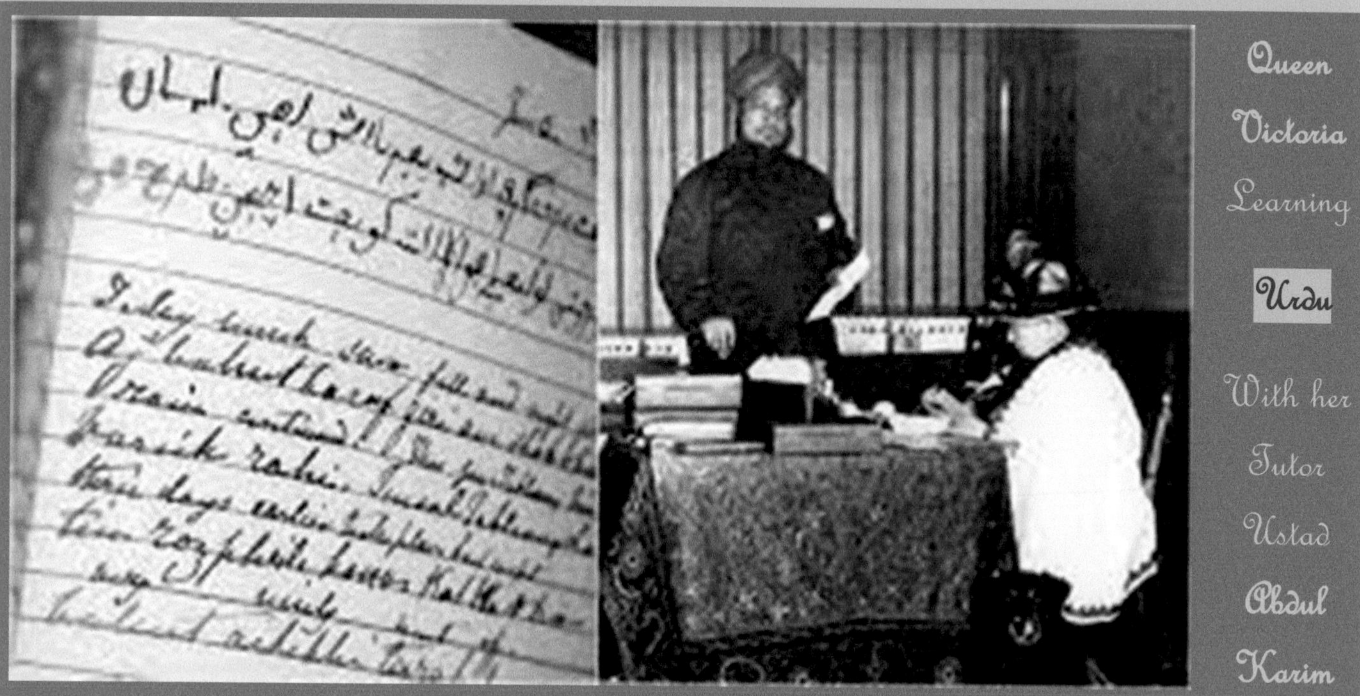

Queen Victoria Learning **Urdu** With her Tutor Ustad **Abdul Karim**

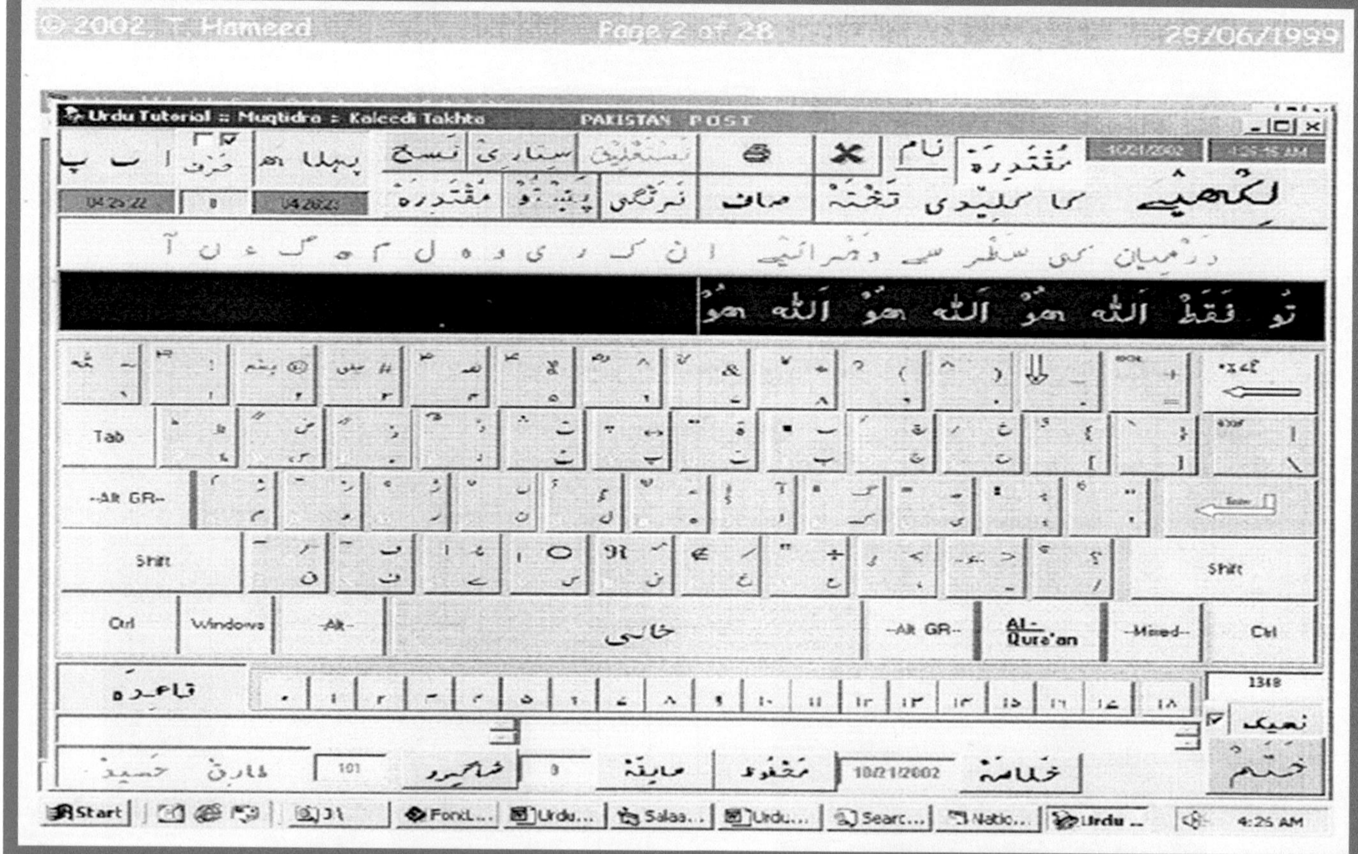

© 2002, T. Hameed
Page 2 of 28
29/06/1999
Urdu Tutorial :: Muqtidra :: Kaleedi Takhta
PAKISTAN POST
Tab
-Alt GR-
Shift
Ctrl
Windows
-Alt-
AL-Qura'an
-Mixed-
Start
4:25 AM

Tariq Hameed ... Digital Numeric Atomic **Urdu-Arabic** ... Wrist Key-Board (1999)

 Page 11 of 24 29/06/1989

اُردُو کی تَرَقّی کی لیے
مُقَتَدِرہ قُومی زُبان (پسنور)
پشاور اور تھرپارکر (تھرپارکر)
سمیت ٹِکنالوجی کے نئے
راستوں کا تَعَیُّن کر رہا ہے

(پ سـ ـو ر) پشـ ـاور اور

Atomic Digital Numerical
Unicode Diacritical Marks
Range: U+0300-036f Imposed

Font ... Digital Numeric Atomic **Urdu-Arabic** ... Quick-Zohar Tariq Hameed Created

۱. بے زیست رہا اس فانی فناء مِیں ... بسا بس نور السَّمٰوات بعد: ۲. جہاں جہاں نہیں اور کہیں نہیں !
ھے تو صرف ، بعد آباد ؛ بعد کے بعد ! ۳. اور جب ہاتھ ہلا الوداع لیے طَارِق ، دنیا کو دنیا مِیں ؟
۴. ہمیش 'آدھا' رہا ! 'سارا' بس بن نہ سکا ... ہزارہا کاوشوں کے بعد ؟

Without Existance was I, in this Fake Universe … Subsisting only in the Lights of the 'Yond 'n of the After:
Where Where was Never 'n Never also Never! What only Was, was Was, After What Was; After the After!
And When, shook Hands with a good Bye, said Tariq, Bye-Bye to the World, herein this World unto?
Ever Forever Remainded only his Worst Half! Never be his Full or Better … Even Thousands Efforts After!

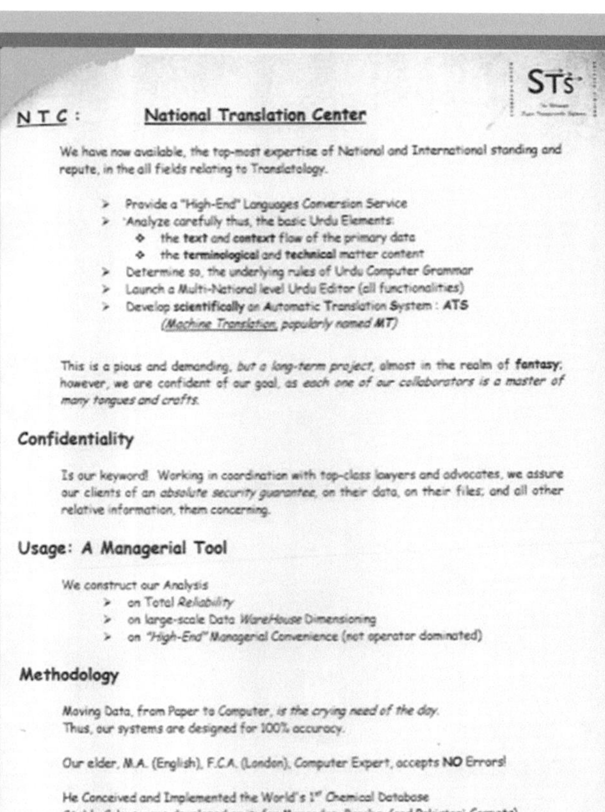

STS

NTC : National Translation Center

We have now available, the top-most expertise of National and International standing and repute, in the all fields relating to Translatology.

- Provide a "High-End" Languages Conversion Service
- Analyze carefully thus, the basic Urdu Elements:
  - the **text** and **context** flow of the primary data
  - the **terminological** and **technical** matter content
- Determine so, the underlying rules of Urdu Computer Grammar
- Launch a Multi-National level Urdu Editor (all functionalities)
- Develop **scientifically** an Automatic Translation System : **ATS** *(Machine Translation, popularly named MT)*

This is a pious and demanding, *but a long-term project*, almost in the realm of **fantasy**; however, we are confident of our goal, *as each one of our collaborators is a master of many tongues and crafts.*

Confidentiality

Is our keyword! Working in coordination with top-class lawyers and advocates, we assure our clients of an *absolute security guarantee*, on their data, on their files; and all other relative information, them concerning.

Usage: A Managerial Tool

We construct our Analysis
- on Total *Reliability*
- on large-scale Data *WareHouse* Dimensioning
- on *"High-End" Managerial Convenience* (not operator dominated)

Methodology

Moving Data, from Paper to Computer, *is the crying need of the day.*
Thus, our systems are designed for 100% accuracy.

Our elder, M.A. (English), F.C.A. (London), Computer Expert, accepts **NO** Errors!

He Conceived and Implemented the World's 1st Chemical Database
Stable Colors were developed on it; for Mercedez, Porche (and Pakistani Carpets)
- BORD: Basic Operational Research Data (CIBA, Switzerland: 1972)
- Innovation: Multi-Relational, Partial Lockings, Automatized Queryings

This was just **short words**. Now, Let us have a **longer talk**.

CHAIRMAN: Dr. Azam Chaudary

CHIEF EXECUTIVE: Tariq Hameed

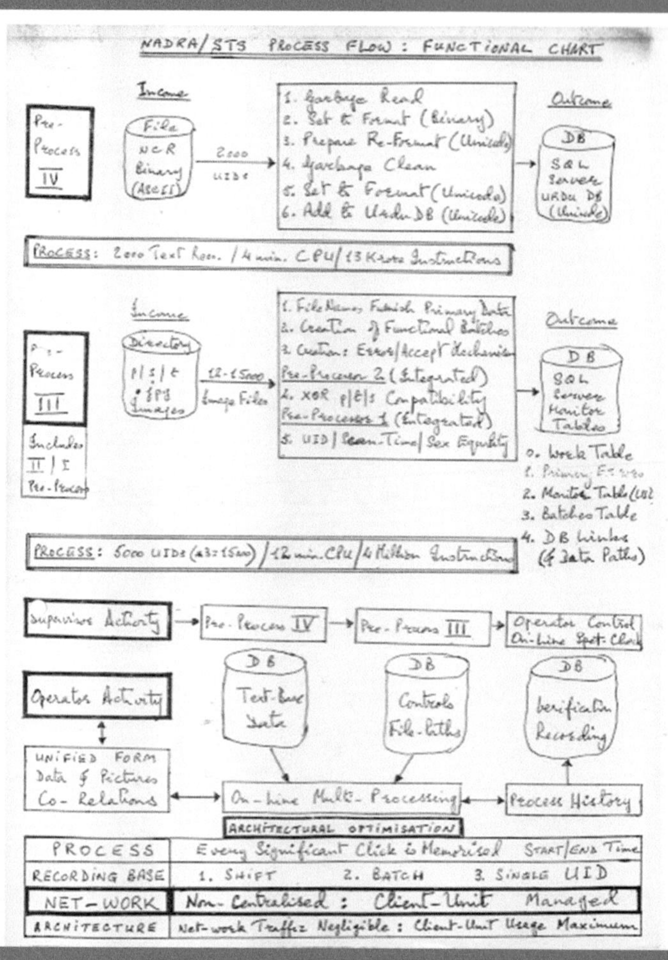

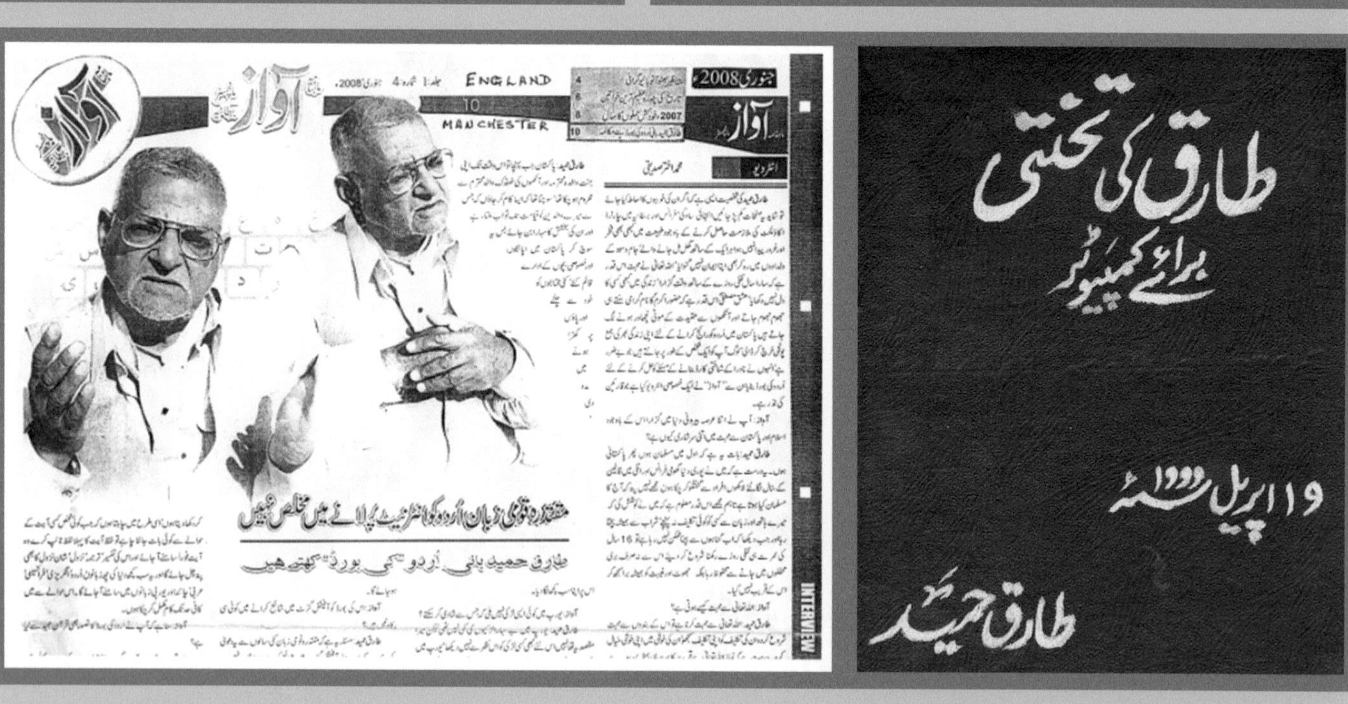

The Honorable Chief Executive

of Our Beloved Country

Respected Sir,

Probably my advice is uncalled for, but I would certainly like to bring up a few points:

1. **Transparence**

The "open declaration" of your tax returns is really commendable. In the betterment of the country, it is a valuable future reference.

Even before, this was a mandatory requirement for politicians in power. Unfortunately, it has never been totally implemented.

In your interest and that of the country, please make this action obligatory in realistic terms. I suggest the following:

- The five top grades of the country (in the administrative sense), either nominated or elected on the national or provincial level, should submit this open tax declaration compulsorily; preferably published in the Official Gazette.
- This declaration should be yearly. An assets variation (specially Incremental), must be likewise attached along with.

2. **Corruption Roots**

- Lack of "Action Transparency" (British Bureaucracy Legacy)
  But then the "Control" was Central (Kingship)
- Limited number of persons (in Cartel Formations)
  Smaller the group, more is it bribable (Lesser Bribe Costs)

In mutual interest of yourself and the country, any type of future parliamentary or decisionary authority, should have much wider and deeper roots, both in national and provincial constitutions. They would consequently be more numerous and samely more difficult to corrupt, because more costly.

3. Khushamdees

Please Be-Aware of "**High-Level**" Pension-Seekers …

History has always proved, that a Well-Intentioned Leader oft is a Prey to the Personal Self Interest "Professional Prætor".

What I call a "Courtier-Clique" now well active in your person are the "Hang-Over" of Older Time: Scrap & Scrub History!

4. Addendum

If you think that a change of the Cultural Environment, as for example, especially bringing-up our Traditional Language as a Tool, Powerful & Workable … can be helpful … on the National & the International Scene, I have some Innovative Methodology & Technology, to expose to your Perusal!

With these few Words,

Your Respected Sir,

I remain truly,

'n Loyally A Private Citizen.

Tariq Hameed : 29/10/1999

thooky@gmail.com

5. Homage to Pak Post

For over 6 months, **Gen Agha** Cordially Invited me to Lodge in his Own Office as DG …

Day & Night I Worked on Urdu & Qura'an Digital Atomisation! "All my Immense Thanks, for a Great Service to the Nation".

General of only 17 ... Tariq-bin-Ziad ... who gave his Name to Gibraltar!

'Tis was a Calm 'n Quiet Eve: three ships folded their Sails 'n glided softly to a stop,, as the Sun Set Sweetly 'n called it a day ... on such a Settling Night! That Night he knew ... that who Controls "**Gibl-ut-Tariq**", Controls the World! **Rocky Mount of Tariq**, thus made History: forever,, as a few Sea-Gulls, headed at ease, Sky-High to their Niches.

In a previous plan, Tariq had already gaged the Spaniard Despotic Usurper Rodrigues' Strength and Weaknesses ... so this time, in 711 he was fully prepared ... he had but a meagre 7000 men against an Armoured Cavalry, esteemed about over 70.000,, thus he had to Plan otherwise: a Clever Tactic, that left not even a suspicion of Defeat!

The night was young 'n Stars Sparkled ... Tariq moved his men to Inner Fortifications ... then in the Calm Sea, at Dawn-break, rose Flames 'n Fire; thus in a matter of minutes, all Ships existed No More; remained Ashes 'n Smoke: No Sails, No Rams, No Planks ... just Ghost Silhouettes of Past Grandeur, Sunk in Waters 'n Waves! Tariq had got up early in the Golden Morn with a few Courageous Friends ... 'n had put ALL to Fire ... **A Path of No Return**!

Then he Spoke: "**F**riends, **F**aithful 'n **F**ighters,, **E**vil **L**ives **S**hort, but **G**lory **L**ives **E**ternally! **Ô**, you People of Belief, where is the Escape? Behind's the Sea 'n Cert Death: but afore you, is Probable Death but Cert Glory,, **DO or DIE**? ▲l-l▲l-l▲ (God) is with you ... and all you Need,, is **Nothing** but **Perseverance 'n Confidence 'n Patience 'n Faith**"!

19th. July, 711 AD, at Wadi-Bakkah (Salado): the demoralized Rodrigues' Army,, immediately shed in blood, was put to flight ... however, Tariq did not Laud his success, but swiftly chased them, for he had realised that Armoured over-loaded **Goth** Cavalry, was No Match for valiant 'n super-speeding horse-men, lightly clad to manoeuvre swift!

Now a few Words about ... the **Boat-Burning Tradition** ... It has existed, 'n was practiced even since Antiquity:

1. Classical figures are believed to destroy ships in brave conquest moments: **Alexander**, **Cæsar**, Apostle **Paul**.
2. Giants of **Gog and Magog**, the Great Perm (North Russia) ... turned out to be a Viking Norse (**Boat Funerals**).
3. This **Gog and Magog** Tradition, carries on in Modern Times (**India**) ... Man, Wife, Belongings (**Sati Funerals**).
4. **Portuguese 'n Spaniards**, Hernán Cortés (Yucatan Peninsula: **1519**) ... expansion activities (**Trading Rituals**).

Rodrigues drowned in River Salado ... 'n thus **Tariq** carried on, his soldiers inspired by his very able Promptness: by the end of 711,, Tariq with his Generals had conquered Cordova up-to Toledo (Gothic Capital),, 'n half Spain ... However, Tariq's Superior, Musa bin Nusair, thinking that Tariq's Forces may-be out-numbered, ordered him not to expand any more: but Tariq, knowing these actual Terrains much better, did not obey; as giving a breath-take to the Enemy, could have been Mortal. So Tariq continued, employing his minimum resources to a maximum advantage!

Musa bin Nusair, highly surprised by the phenomenal successes of Tariq, simultaneously landed in Spain with his supporting army ... however, at first, he was truly displeased by Tariq's dis-obedience,, but seeing the true ground Realities, forgave him magnanimously: **to carry on the Spanish Conquest**! After dominating Savilla, he joined Tariq in Toledo,, to carry on to the high-lands of Leon, Aragon and Galicia. Consequently, in only under two years, the two Muslims Veterans, had brought most of Northern Spain, up till the Pyrenees, under their authority!

Musa received peremptory orders of the Caliph Walid, that with his Lieutenant **Tariq**, they present themselves in Damascus,, where, on their arrival in the Umayyed Capital, in Feb 715, received with due decorum 'n honour, as Heroes deserve! Unfortunately, the Caliph died soon after: replaced by his brother Suleman, **resentful 'n jealous of their success**! Historians say, that the two Glorious Generals were Humiliated and Dis-Honoured,, to be left on the Streets, in Need 'n in Want ... 'n so is How they Perished ... **for Services Rendered to the Meaner of the Mean**!

The Mean NEVER ... but **the GREAT Leave always a Name in History**!

General of only 17 ... Tariq-bin-Ziad ... who gave his Name to Gibraltar!

Origins of Tariq ... was he a Berber,, was he a Moroccan,, was he an Arab ... None seems to know? What one knows is that **he was**: with a Name from the Qura'an ... 'n that's what Counts "**Gibl-ut-Tariq**",, **Boat-Burner**!

Character of Tariq ... he possessed an Indomitable Courage,, 'n strong Will-Power,, full Strength 'n Stamina ... his Confidence 'n Faith were Infallible,, 'n his Plans were Brilliantly Conceived 'n Harmoniously Executed,, 'n his Military Strategies were Swift 'n Intrepid ... He was Mature 'n Self-Disciplined 'n Cool 'n Balanced in Mind, in All 'n Every Adverse or Favourable Circumstances ... 'n **Totally a Self-Master**, in Face of the Strongest of Oppositions!

Personality of Tariq ... his Fine Personality had many Humanitarian Aspects ... Dignified, Self-Restrained, Devout to All 'n his Cause, totally Un-Mindful of Who Thought What of What he did,, but that **Be it Well-Done** ... Respectful to his Superiors, Courteous to his Equals 'n Kind 'n Considerate to his Inferiors ... One of the very few in History, who have left a **Hall-Mark of Character,, of Intelligence, of Bounty, 'n of Simplicity in Pure Goodness**!

Finally ... to Sum Up ... **Frailty, Thy Name is Woman** ... (Hamlet: Shakespeare)

10000 Sages Tortured,, **mul.mul.Mullaism** ... **Treason, Thyne Name is Pride** ... (Me: Shake-a-Pear)

Gibraltar's History ... Small Peninsula in Southern Iberia ... as Mediterranean Opens ...

https://unsplash.com/s/photos/gibraltar
photo-1595353022520-93a6386e0b16.jpg

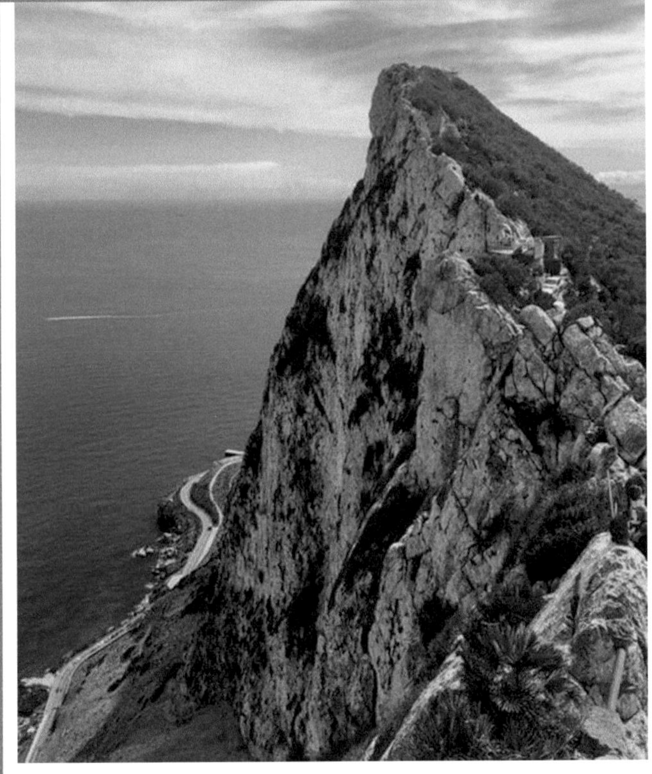

https://unsplash.com/s/photos/gibraltar
photo-1571081523650-af92f468af65.jpg

History spans over 2,900 years ... of reverence in ancient times ... to "the most **dense, fortified, contested European Point**". **Gibraltar**: populated 50,000 years ago by Neanderthals, ended around 24,000, at their disappearance. After came Phoenicians, Carthaginians, Romans: belief & worship of the **Twin Pillars Hercules Shrines** ... **Gibraltar Rock** 'Hollow Rock', *Mons Calpe*!

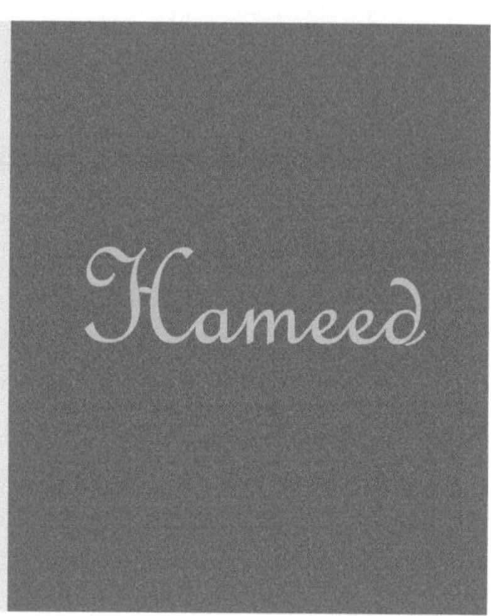

Voracious Reader 'n Searcher, since Two 'n Half years Old, of Where **LIES** the **TRUTH**?

"**Aye, there lies the rub**": so in this Hamlet of No Return, called 'World of the Wise Men of Gotham', but Bed-Ridden by the Un-Wise of Bottom, my small Wisdom but Swore faintly; "**Never Truly Grow-up**"!

'Twas Destiny, that born Myopic, forced me to **Imagine**. Thus, Truth 'n Purity came to Grasp: it dawned that, "Dirt were you Born, to returnest to Dirt" ... **Empty-Handed Come, 'n Empty-Handed Gone** ... thus lil by lil, formed a Philosophy: "**You only GAIN, what you GIVE**"! Help Humanity; Not your own Self-Self!

Surprisingly, I learned early, that **Seeing was Un-Truth** ... Lampions big of Light, Blinking 'n Flickering, so Blown-up in Multi-Fluid Colours in the Depths of Cosmos' ... factually were, **Else-Things in Else-Where**? Questions to be Posed 'n Answered: allowing the use of other Senses, like Sounds, Taste, Smell 'n Movements,, 'n thus to Re-construct the **Probable Reality**; intuitively analysing the crayoned cricks 'n cracks of chalky traits, I Heard the Black-Board Talk back to me: 'n Revealed by Magic, the **Writing on the Wall** ... 'n so Un-Veiled so fully, the Falsehood of the **Persons of Convenience**?

Only pictures 'n books were my Mates. Actually, Mental Correction always rectifying the Worldly Vision ... suddenly Adult, one put Glasses on my Nose? Help! Ahhhh, the Truth: which I already knew since so long, by books 'n looks: 'n my dear Ancient Masters, who had made my Imagination, my Best Friend, for-ever!

Friends! Live to Give ... Fill Graves with Souls, NOT Soles ... Tread down, in Here-After?

Ever Be True: the Mental Remains 'n Captures All as a Pure Child ... Never as Sallied Humans: who in Truth are, Not **Sapiens**, but **Serf-Peons**! Slaves of the Junky-Jungle-Law: Lead by the Lowly Mi-Lords; by Law?

Sink the Beast, to Save the Sky-Bid Angels ... To be or not to be, that's the Question!

Write 'n Put 25 years in a Drawer. If U find, it still good? It Might have some Value in it ... T. S. Eliot.

... **TARIQ** ... ONLY PERSON IN WORLD ... WAITING TO PUBLISH TILL 80 ...

... **TARIQ** ... ONLY PERSON IN WORLD ... WAITING TO PUBLISH TILL 80 ...

Publishing Planned: 21/02/2021 1st. book **Completion: 05/02/2021**

(**Mother's Goodbye-World Anniversary ... '72**) Kublai Khan (**Kublai Coronation ... 05/05/1260**)

History of **Urdu** ... The **Mongol**/Turkish word **Urdu** means "**Camp**" or "**Palace**" ... Kublai ...

... **The Final Place of Rest** ... And That's How My Poëm Ends: Sadly ...

Awaiting; that the Loose last breath, be shed,
'N downed he slept: Camp Urdu in bed,
That Spirits to the Ninth Heaven Arise.

That.Spirits.to.the.Ninth.Heaven.Arise...

Beethoven's.9th.Sympohony.first.recording.(Bruno.Seidler-Winkler,1923)

Beethoven's.9th.Sympohony.(Hymn.to.Joy)...https://www.youtube.com/watch?v=nZV2EuA9fwM

Publishing Planned: 05/05/2021 2nd. book **Completion: 14/08/2021**

(**Kublai Khan's Coronation ... 05/05/1260**) 'tween 9 'n 15 (**Pak Independence ... 14/08/1947**)

Publishing Planned: 05/05/2021 3rd. book ... 3-1 **Completion: 29/10/2021**

(**Kublai Khan's Coronation ... 05/05/1260**) Tayles 'Tween Struts 'n Frets ... 1 (**Myne Birth-Date ... 29/10/1941**)

An Emperor, Leaning on Staff of his Wealth: Humiliated, Us Poor Souls' Love, by Stealth? Taj Mahal ... Akbar Allahbadi ... اکبر الہبادی https://www.pexels.com/photo/black-and-white-photo-of-the-taj-mahal-7582485/	اک شہنشاہ نے دولت کا سہارا لے کر: ہم غریبوں کی محبت کا اڑایا ہے مزاق ؟	

Printed in the United States
by Baker & Taylor Publisher Services